THE DIFFERENCE
BETWEEN

TRUTH AND OPINION

HOW THE MISUSE OF LANGUAGE CAN LEAD TO DISASTER

TIMOTHY J. COONEY

PROMETHEUS BOOKS
BUFFALO, NEW YORK

104266

For
Beth Preddy

Published 1991 by Prometheus Books

editorial offices at 700 East Amherst Street, Buffalo, New York 14215; distribution facilities at 59 John Glenn Drive, Amherst, New York 14228

Library of Congress Cataloging-in-Publication Data

Cooney, Timothy J.
    The difference between truth and opinion : how the misuse of language can lead to disaster / by Timothy J. Cooney.
        p.   cm.

    ISBN 0-87975-668-3
    1. Truth. 2. Opinion. 3. Analysis. 4. Ethics. I. Title.
BC171.C66   1991
160—dc20   90-23842
                                                                            CIP

Printed on acid-free paper in the United States of America

The difference between truth and
  opinion.

Contents

PART TWO: RELIGION, MORALITY, AND
              LINGUISTIC CHAOS

Acknowledgments

I can perhaps best explain what I owe to various people by first presenting my argument and its genesis in a nutshell. I try to show that:

> how we talk effects how we think and feel;
>
> if we talked differently, we would think and feel differently;
>
> the easiest thing to change is how we talk.

Is change in order? In my opinion, yes. I believe that how we now talk—the very words and grammatical forms we naturally and instinctively employ—is needlessly infuriating.

This belief was originally generated when I tried to analyze my own angers. Looking back I guess they were no more or less intense than average, but I came to look upon them with a suspicion bordering on paranoia. Who put these angers in me? What was their motivation? Why am I angry at this and not at that, which so angers you? I came to feel that I was a Pavlovian dog that had been trained to growl and bite by word commands. I came to fear all messages beyond the level of "Pass the salt" and "Nice day, huh?"

I came to believe that on this overcrowded, polluted, religious, and armed-to-the-teeth planet it is more important how we talk than what we say.

By way of restlessly experimenting on my nascent ideas and trying to reduce my own angers, I began—about fifteen years ago— talking in a way quite different from the way I used to talk or the way other people I knew talked. For one thing, I put the word "opinion" in front of a lot of my messages, in particular declaratives that I could not verify by my senses. I also developed a halting way of arguing that highlighted the uncertainty I felt toward my own beliefs and decisions, both major and minor.

In time, some of my friends started copying the way I talked, at least when they were talking to me. At first it was a humorous mimicking of all my uncertainties, but in time it became more natural. And if I failed to include the word "opinion" when it was considered in order, howls of protest were set off, like the reaction to a stickler for etiquette who tackles his or her chop with the salad fork.

These were fun and heady days, like a new parlor game suddenly taking off, and I was the author!

One young friend said she felt much less angry with the world and the people in it—including her husband—since she had started putting the word "opinion" in front of most of her beliefs. She suggested that we make opinion a religion. Another friend cried out: "Opinionates of the world unite!" And still another said that uttering the word "opinion" was like the "om" of yoga, a mind relaxer.

I remember getting a call one morning around two from a new acquaintance who had had a few too many, and he delivered a run-on sentence that went something like this: "There comes a magic moment when something you believe to be true with all your heart is recognized as only a matter of opinion and the other guy is not crazy or evil because he doesn't agree with you and your angers wither for without truth to support them they are just tantrums and you feel healthier and you see a lot of your fellow man is no more screwed up than you . . . lovely, lovely, you should write a book and call it the *Magic Moment*." I laughed and was encouraged and went back to sleep.

Then I had a disintegrating experience. Someone said: "In *my opinion* arson is immoral!"

"No, no," I cried, frightened and instinctively, "arson is not a matter of opinion!"

"Are you saying you can verify it is wrong?"

"Well . . ." My stomach fell so fast it left a vacuum; it was a horrible moment, like that moment when—at the age of six—a classmate questioned the existence of God. I saw my ideas unraveling.

This experience sent me to the wilderness for five years. If I could not show that the arson declarative should *not* have the word "opinion" in front of it, then I had better stop fooling around with the word. The world was in deep enough trouble without making arson a matter of opinion.

Eventually, however, things worked out; I discovered that the arson declarative is true and can be verified by our senses and should not have the word "opinion" in front of it. Do I realize the enormity or preposterousness of what I have just written? I do. It's a short book, so please don't drop it now because you *know* I must be crazy. I promise to show you that the arson declarative is verifiable by our senses and it won't be by any smoke or mirrors or any special use of traditional terms. Nor will it be that arson is morally wrong "by definition"—arson is illegal by definition, but not immoral by definition.

In time, I began to write. But repeatedly I would show my writing to friends and they despaired: "I don't get it. You're making it too complicated. Write like you talk." And I would answer: "I'm trying, but the distinction between truth and opinion is not that damn simple—when you think about it."

I considered giving up a number of times, not because I couldn't get at the distinction, but because it was complicated and I felt I could not hope for a widely read book. And without this hope, what was the sense? The book would be academic.

But what haunted me and brought me back to the screen was that the distinction wasn't all that complicated. If I could reach a certain amount of people who would talk differently because of my argument, they in turn might have an impact—by the way they talked—on the larger population, whom I could not hope to reach directly.

Now, then, to my acknowledgments. Beth Preddy's contributions were so many that at one point I suggested that she be coauthor. She declined on the grounds that the ideas were mine and that however much she was helping me in shaping them, she would not feel comfortable being coauthor. My own view is that the ideas never would have taken shape were it not for our endless talks and her tireless reading of the manuscript. In any case, she would have been coauthor, had she agreed. She is now working on a book on morality for grade school children and is using the ideas in the second half of this book, so it all may come out even in the end.

Almost from the beginning, Tom Morgan read drafts of the manuscript at various stages. He is the sort of friend who is so encouraging that if, on occasion, I sent him material and he did not respond, I would just send him some more, certain that he did not mean to slight me, but that he was just busy on more pressing matters. And time and again he did respond.

Along the way, Jim Haughton read several drafts of the full manuscript, and parts of it many times. His method of criticism was wonderful and unique in my experience. He would take pages out, hand them back to me and say "Here, here's your argument, forget the other stuff. It belongs in some other book. Just build on this." And each time, I saw my argument more clearly.

During the summer of 1988, Peter and Lee Schoenberg read the complete manuscript and made many notes, most of which I took to heart. They also suggested striking out two preliminary chapters, and I followed this suggestion as well.

My debt to these five people is immeasurable.

In early 1989, I had a few linguistic puzzles that were torturing me, so I wrote to Professor Noam Chomsky at the Massachusetts Institute of Technology. I did not know him personally but I had heard that he was friendly (*academica amicus*). Hearsay proved correct, and he solved or dissolved my problems in a way that made me smile.

In the spring of 1989, I again wrote to Professor Chomsky to ask if he knew a graduate student who might be interested in critiquing my manuscript. He passed my letter on to Professor Sylvain Bromberger, who in turn put Prescott W. Smith in touch with me.

This contact proved to be a wonderful piece of good luck. Mr. Smith traversed so well that delicate line between nit picking my ideas to death and pointing out serious errors and confusions. He was a delight to work with and is one of the most intelligent people I have run across.

If my publisher, Dr. Paul Kurtz, is not the last Renaissance person, he is certainly one of a handful of them, and may be their leader. Prometheus's list of titles reflects his excitements and enjoyments and is as broad as it is enlightening. Paul teaches, lectures, debates, writes, and is a freethinker and a free spirit. I am very proud to be a guest in the house that he built.

A writer—I cannot recall who it was—once said: "I read the works of others to see what I can get away with." My editor, Steven L. Mitchell, is one of the most urbane and widely read people I have met, and so when he says "You can't get away with that," "This does not make sense," or "This needs clarifying," it seldom crosses my mind to argue with him. I am sure he is right by the ineffable, albeit ineluctable, standards of clear writing. The weird and awkward usages that remain in this book are therefore strictly mine by insistence; I use them to break the tedium and to make my contribution to what one can (or cannot) get away wit.

I now come to the most difficult part of these acknowledgments, recognizing those who have helped to a lesser degree. Worse yet I know I will accidentally leave someone out. Included in this list are people who never saw my manuscript in any form but who at some point in time listened to my ideas and made suggestions: Hugh Abramson, Ronnie Asbell, Lorraine Baranski, Roger Becker, Toshii Booth, Clarence Bruner-Smith, Kenneth Burke, Marc Campbell, Stephanie Carlloti, Chris Cooney, John R. Day, Jane Dietrich, Mohammed Ekmekji, Jason Epstein, Jennifer Greiner, Sy Gru, Laurie Gutierrez, Sidney Hook, Larry Johnson, George Karanski, Imok Kim, Ben Kremen, Jonathan Lieberson, Harry Martens, Vincent Mosso, Barbara Miller, Shaw Muscat, Debs Myers, Gloria Ohnmeis, George Ouzounian, Louis R. Paret, Ray Robinson, A. M. Rosenthal, Judy Rothman, Ranjit Sandhu, Amaud Saud, Peter Singer, Leslie Slote, Annie Sprinkle, and Robert F. Wagner.

My intellectual debts could go on for many pages, but any listing would include in a rough order of their influence on me: A. J. Ayer, Ludwig Wittgenstein, G. E. Moore, and Bertrand Russell.

For writing style and clarity of expression there are two books that I read over and over: F. Scott Fitzgerald's *The Great Gatsby* and Carl Becker's *The Heavenly City of the Eighteenth-Century Philosophers.* If the latter is unfamiliar, well, in my opinion, it is exposition at its finest.

I am a major character in two works of fiction and maybe the word "character" should be underlined. Some friends say I was treated badly by the authors, but I loved the portrayals and thought them to be for the most part accurate. That I have feet, ankles, and knees of clay does not preclude the fact that I like myself for being able to spot an opinion being palmed off as a truth, and correcting or alerting my neighbors. The works are: *Houses Without Porches* by N. Shaam Krasner and *Wild Oats* by Jacob Epstein.

Last, but most important, there is Joan Ganz Cooney, my ex-wife, who has supported me financially for many years and who has been my most trusted voice of reason. This book would not be without her, and I doubt that I would either. *Variety* always refers to her as St. Joan, to which I say Amen (she is the head of the Children's Television Workshop and is the creator of "Sesame Street"). She is the the kindest person one is likely to meet in a dozen and a half lifetimes.

Manhattan   January 1991

Preface

The purpose of this book is to reduce the amount of anger in the world by about half. How much effect this would have on the amount of violence I won't predict, although clearly there is a relationship between anger and violence.

My method is linguistic analysis. In the beginning was the word, which was closely followed, we can be sure, by the first linguistic mistake. And ever since, people have been making mistakes and correcting one another: e.g., "That's not called a 'cat,' it's called a 'dog.' "

I believe that a tremendous amount of anger is generated by the innocent confusion of truth with opinion; an error we fail to correct often enough but could get in the habit of correcting (and not making) more often if we possessed a better understanding of the difference between these two concepts.

It is easy to take a cynical view of humankind. We live in a world where selfish desires are in fierce conflict, and we use and abuse language to get what we want. Yet the cynical view, while it may often be justified, does not account for the major slaughters of history where masses of innocent people run off wildly to kill other masses of innocents with no hope of personal gain.

When it comes to rage and mass slaughter I believe there is something at work that has been overlooked, namely, a passionate, primeval, primordial defense of truth. This is not to say that most of us don't lie on occasion, but rather that we become fierce defenders of truth when someone lies to us or rejects the truth.

Let a child reject the truth about matches and his parents will hammer the truth into his head. Let the worst liar and cheat among us be, in truth, shortchanged, and watch his righteous rage. Even little slips of the tongue are quickly corrected if not by the speaker, then by the listener, lest a nontruth pass into the void uncorrected.

So what's the point of all this? My point is that naturally, psychologically, passionately, and primordially we become just as furious when defending an opinion that we believe is a truth. Yet, let an opinion be recognized for what it is and—poof!—all the steam goes out of us. Who, for example, would go to war under the banner "In our opinion we are right!" or "We think God may be on our side"?

As the would-be psychiatrist must go through analysis before entering practice, so you, my gentle reader, must purge yourself of all opinion implanted in your brain as truth. It will be painful at times but the rewards are great.

You will, in time, be able to gently collapse the arguments of those who refuse to make the distinction between truth and opinion. The procedures I teach are insidious, more akin to an attack by a virus than a sledgehammer. A word here, a question there and you will create uncertainty, precursor of poof.

My promise to you is that in the end you will feel so refreshed, so free, so relieved of ancient junk, that you will joyously apply the procedures on everyone you meet.

What is my book, truth or opinion? I believe my basic argument is capable of verification by our senses, in particular listening to language and observing the rage that is engendered when opinion is expressed as truth.

I think it is fair to say that philosophers and linguists are in general agreement that there are at least two kinds of verified truths: the truths of pure math and empirical truths.

I also think it is fair to say that there has been a search for a third kind of truth but that there has been no general agreement on its nature. Some have called it *intuitive truth,* but intuition suffers from a big problem: if I intuit one way and you intuit another way, where are we?

I believe that there is a third kind of truth—a devilishly tricky fellow to identify and isolate because it is usually expressed in a few simple words, yet its unspoken, background argument is long and intricate. It is a truth about the best way to satisfy a specific desire. I call this message the "desire declarative."

Examples of these three different kinds of truth are:

"Two and two are four."
"Interstate 80 links San Francisco and New York City."
"Interstate 80 is the right road."

All three messages could be true, but the third can only be true if we desire to go somewhere and Interstate 80 takes us there. The desire declarative is the foundation of my argument.

Part One

Truth, Opinion, and the Phony Declarative

Chapter One

Decisions, Decisions

Language is a vast, rich, subtle, bewitching, sublime, and grand business. My interest is in a narrow area of it, an area where I believe more anger and violence are created by innocently confusing truth and opinion than in any other area. I am not interested in language as it is used to tell stories, create poetry, criticize, report, philosophize, comfort, gossip, complain, or, that most mysterious usage, to tell jokes. My interest is in language as it is used in decision-making situations. These decisions include:

> decisions that affect two or more people; personal decisions where the speaker is asking for information or advice; and decisions about what to teach children.

Here are some questions that might arise in such discourse:

Can you tell me which road I take to get to San Francisco?

Do you think I should hire Jones for the job?

Should we ski at Stowe this weekend?

What should we tell our child about sex, religion, and drugs?

What should we do with the thief in our midst?

Should society allow abortion?

Should society build nuclear power plants?

Should our country go to war?

Should I go to war?

Let me now further narrow my area of interest, define some terms, and give you a rough idea of my argument in Part One.

LIES AND LIARS

Within decision discourse there is a fertile and fascinating subdivision that, for the most part, I will not explore—specifically, the deceptive use of language to effect decisions and to get what one wants. I won't claim for those I cite in my examples that they are trying to be fiercely honest; only that what they are saying, they believe to be true. Looked at another way, I am less interested in those who lie and lead than those who believe and follow, i.e., people like you and me, the traditional cannon fodder.

THE BACKGROUND ARGUMENT

Most of the messages we exchange in decision discourse are in an extremely abbreviated shorthand. The reason is simple enough. We are in a hurry to reach a decision and to satisfy the desire at stake; unnecessary words cost time and can irritate the listener.

Let's take a simple example. John and Marsha* are on their way to Boston by car, but something has gone wrong with the engine. Ordinarily, Marsha would be trying to fix the problem since she is more knowledgeable about cars, but her wrist is in a cast. So John is doing the actual work under her direction.

At one point John asks "Which wrench?" and Marsha replies "Three eighth's!"

They issue these messages as opposed to: "Which wrench should I use given my desire to get these bolts off?" "The wrench marked with the fraction three-eighth's is the one you want given your desire to get those bolts off!"

I call the extended explanation behind the spoken words the *background argument.*

---

*I have taken these names from the party record "John and Marsha" (Sunshine Specials, Chicago, 1927); a record of considerable linguistic significance. Only two messages are exchanged ("John" and "Marsha"), but they are exchanged 36 times. Yet, by inflection and emphasis, each message is made different.

The record starts out with a cheerful exchange, "John . . . Marsha," leading through an accusatory "John!" followed by a guttural, pleading "Marsha . . . ," to a climactic "John!!!! . . . Marsha!!!!" The point is that inflection and emphasis can also convey information, further shortening the number of words that have to be spoken.

STANDARD MESSAGE FORMS

One way we are able to reduce the amount of spoken words is through what I call *standard message forms*. I mean, for example, that *the very order* in which words are spoken can convey different background arguments, e.g., "There is life on Mars!" versus "Is there life on Mars?" The inclusion of a key word or phrase can also create unique forms, e.g., *"In my opinion* there is other life in the universe." Or compare "This is butter!" with "This is *like* butter."

The two forms of vital concern to my argument are

> *The bold, declarative forms:**
>
> "The world is round!"
>
> "This is the road to Boston!"
>
> *The opinion form:*
>
> "In my opinion we should not send
> men and women to Mars."
>
> "In my opinion Route 12 is quicker."

In decision-making situations the bold, declarative form is used to express what the speaker feels certain is true. (Or, in the case of liars, what the speaker wants the listener to believe is true.) The opinion form is used to express uncertainty. It is created by taking a bold declarative and weakening it with the insertion of specific phrases: "in my opinion . . . ," "I think . . . ," or "I believe. . . ."

---

*In the examples I call upon, I will always end messages that are in the bold, declarative form with an exclamation point. In the cast of actual exclamations or imperatives, I will use a double exclamation point.

THE COMPELLING POWER
OF THE DECLARATIVE FORM

Given the effect it can have on people, the bold, declarative form is the most powerful form we can employ in decision discourse. "Stowe has a foot of snow!" can virtually compel people to the mountain if they want to ski. Indeed, all over the states of New York, Massachusetts, Connecticut, Vermont, and New Hampshire scores of people—like ants on instinct—are virtually being compelled to Stowe because they have received this little snippet of a message, this verbal cameo of "snow at Stowe."

If the Stowe declarative is not true, it will still compel people to the bare mountain and provoke blind rage when they arrive, which is to hint that the bold declarative should be handled cautiously. The form is compelling whether it be true, partially true, untrue, or a matter of opinion.

HOW DO DECLARATIVES ACTUALLY COMPEL US?

It's hard to say, but I have found the following idea to be helpful: The bold declarative generates a picture of part of the world (snow at Stowe) in the mind of the listener;* the listener looks at the picture and sees how to get what he wants; he lays out a course of action and then moves out smartly into the real world. Or he does nothing . . . if there is no snow at Stowe.

That all this may only take milliseconds would only surprise pre-computer generations and those who have never experienced a dream.

What I like about this idea is that even if it is not the way

---

*The "picture theory of language" is Wittgenstein's (*passim*) and there is no doubt his theory sparked mine.

the mind works, I still think we must be able to paint a picture when we are presented with a bold declarative in decision discourse. If we can't, there may be something seriously wrong with the message such that it should not be in the bold, declarative form.

THE EASIEST THING IN THE WORLD

The easiest thing in the world to do is to take what is actually an opinion and put it in the bold declarative form. For example, just drop the first three words in this message: "*In my opinion* puce is the right color for the reception area" and voilà, you have a message in the bold, declarative form.

Nevertheless, it's still an opinion *despite its form.* It is *an opinion masquerading as a truth.* Or, to be more technical, it is a phony declarative; a message in the bold, declarative form that is other than true.

THE ARGUMENT OF PART ONE

If I had to put the argument of Part One in a sentence, it would be: *The bold declaratives we issue in decision discourse must be true if our intention is not to confuse, delay, deceive, or infuriate.*

"What do you mean by true?!!"
"I mean messages in the bold, declarative form that have been verified by our senses."*

---

*The one exception to this definition of "true" is the truths of pure math, which are not verified by our senses. Relatively speaking they seldom arise in decision discourse, and I will formally set them aside in the next chapter.

USE OF THE WORD "LEGITIMATE"

When I use the word "legitimate" I mean nonconfusing, e.g., "In decision discourse the only legitimate declarative is a true declarative."

SOME BOLD DECLARATIVES

Here are some messages in the bold, declarative form that I will be examining:

"Interstate 80 links San Francisco and New York City!"

"Roger is the wrong person for the job!"

"It is wrong to play with matches!"

"It is wrong to play with yourself!"

"Stealing is wrong!"

"Arson is wrong!"

"Abortion is wrong!"

"Abortion is a basic right!"

"This is a just war!"

All of these messages are grammatically correct. A lot of them look virtually alike. Most of them have a similar cadence when spoken aloud. And any one of them might be voiced by someone who is sane and certain that what he or she is saying is true.

Despite their similarities I will try to show that what we have here is a mishmosh of messages founded *on substantively different kinds of background arguments.*

Reason and common sense suggest that if the background arguments are *that* different, then the words, and the forms used to express them, should not look and sound so much alike, if our intention is not to confuse, infuriate, or drive one another mad.

Put bluntly, I shall try to show that some of these messages are phony declaratives; they don't belong in the declarative form since they are not true.

But how can we tell which is which? By going to their background arguments.

LINGUISTIC SURGERY

As the would-be surgeon learns his or her quick and deft cutting by long practice on dead things, so in Part One we will be dissecting the background arguments of lifeless declaratives; ones about right wrenches and wrong roads. Messages put in the declarative form are difficult enough to open up and explore without having any emotional attachment to them.

However, like a novice surgeon, you should get faster at the cutting as you get more practice, and should soon be able to open up any message, including those at the center of our most violent confrontations.

To be more specific, I will teach you some questions to ask of any message that should quickly expose the background argument and separate true messages from opinion messages, regardless of what form they are put in.

Then, in Part Two we will enter the most serious area of decision discourse—life-and-death decisions that pass under the headings of morality, religion, and politics. It is an area as fascinating as it is frightening; an area teeming with phony declaratives, threatening at any moment to compel whole populations on slaughtering rampages against evil. To complicate matters there is, in truth, such a thing as evil, but it is not as widespread as we have led ourselves to believe through our linguistic mistakes.

In Part One I shall begin by examining declaratives that are true. They will serve as our benchmark for defining and exploring opinion. Then I shall finish Part One with a look at some simple, phony declaratives.

Chapter Two

Only Three Kinds of Truths

There are, I believe, three kinds of truths. Let's begin by setting one kind aside: those of pure math. It has been said of these declaratives that they are not verified by our senses but by appeal to self-evident first principles.

I find this explanation troublesome, but I have seen none better and I have no need to vent my troubles since these declaratives seldom arise in decision discourse. When they do arise they seldom make trouble: "Four and four are eight!" "I can't argue with you there!"

The second kind of bold declarative is known under various names and is universally celebrated because it includes among its members the truths of science. It is a declarative that tells us something about the physical world, and I call it the physical-world declarative (PWD). It is an empirical truth verified by our senses.

Finally, there is a little orphan fellow that, so far as I know, has gone unrecognized these past four or five thousand years. It, too, is an empirical truth yet it is much different from the physical-world declarative or the truths of science. I call it the desire declarative (DD). It is a message that tells the listener the best way to satisfy, or not frustrate, a specific desire: e.g., "Route 1 is the right road!" "Route 2 is the wrong road!"

Unlike the physical-world declarative, the desire declarative is only found in decision discourse. "This is the right wrench!" makes no sense unless we want something and have a decision to make.

The DD is my main concern, but by way of setting the stage and developing some terminology let us first examine its celebrated sibling, the PWD.

Chapter Three

The Physical-World Declarative

"Interstate 80 links New York City and San Francisco!" means that if we leave New York City on I-80, then—in time—we will *see* a city that everyone *calls* San Francisco! And vice versa if we leave from San Francisco. If this is what we see and hear, then we may say of this message—this bold declarative—that it has been verified by our senses. "What I saw you will see, too!"

If this declarative has been verified, then we may pass it on to others who, in turn, may pass it on without verifying it. Soon the I-80 declarative is in general circulation, issued by people who have not personally verified it, yet causing no trouble—because it has been verified. It's like a gold coin.

Furthermore, we may say of such declaratives that they are true.

31

Which is to suggest that the word "true" has a quite precise meaning: verified by our senses.

And the word "truth" is just a noun that stands for a true message.*

We may also say of true messages or truths that they are facts. Thus:

"Tom only has one leg!"

"Yes, what you say is:

"a true message,

"a truth,

"a fact,

---

*The etymologies of the words "true" and "truth" are interesting with respect to decision discourse. The adjective "true" existed before the noun "truth." In fact, the "th" in "truth" was the Old English way of creating nouns out of adjectives, which is to say that, historically, the interesting word is "true" and not "truth."

Originally, "true" meant steadfast or trustworthy; this strongly suggests that its original use was as an adjective qualifying *messengers* rather than messages: "Uglug says the rabbits are back on the hill and the bear has gone to its den!" "Is she trustworthy, steadfast, true?" "Yes, Uglug is most true, steadfast, trustworthy!" "Good!! So then, with the bear in its lair let's hurry to the hill and hunt hare."

Only in time did the word "true" come to qualify messages: "Was what she said true?" "Yes, what she said was true." Obviously, if Uglug's message was not true, or if it was true and someone rejected it, rage would be but a step away since the hunters might miss a meal or become one.

Eventually, messages that were true received their own noun: "truth." Subsequently, everything but the kitchen sink got called "true" and "truth," causing rage and mass slaughterings, among other things.

"a legitimate declarative,

"a verified declarative . . . I verified it
myself when Tom and I went swimming."

THE PHYSICAL-WORLD DECLARATIVE
EXPRESSES NEAR CERTAINTY

Imagine that you are a first-time visitor to New York City and
you ask me—your friend and a longtime resident of N.Y.C.—where
Madison Square Garden is located. I issue the following declarative: "Madison Square Garden is at 33rd Street and Eighth Ave-
nue!" Is my message true? Yes, I have verified it many times. Is
it *absolutely true* that if you go to 33rd and Eighth, you will see
MSG? No. Like all physical-world declaratives, the MSG declarative is only a near-certainty message. Or, looked at another way,
it is *a high probability message.*

Buildings can burn down, fall down, be moved, erode, and
explode. It is even *possible* that the moon—severed by an intragalactic pi string—might not be in its customary place tomorrow.
Indeed, over the years Madison Square Garden has been at three
different locations in Manhattan.

Furthermore, our eyes can play tricks on us, our memories
can fail, and there can be typos on maps and in phone books.
So should I have said: "MSG is probably at 33rd and Eighth"
or "I think it is at 33rd and Eighth"?

No—assuming that I am as sure of its location as I am of anything else in the physical world.

Indeed, if I am sure, then I *must* use the declarative form,
assuming my intention is not to delay you.

Why? Because this form already takes into account the totally unexpected. If I weaken my declarative by qualifying it, I may

delay you, as you feel you must check with someone else as to the whereabouts of MSG.

UNCERTAINTY MUST BE EXPRESSED

When we want to express near certainty there is this handy short form we can use—the declarative form. We don't have to say "It is true that the world is round!" rather we can just issue the last four words; the form takes care of the rest.

But there is no short form to express uncertainty. If I am not sure where Madison Square Garden is or if I know that it is in the process of being relocated but am uncertain of the details, then I must speak out the degree of my uncertainty ranging from "I am almost sure . . ." through "I think . . ." to "I don't know for sure, but if I had to guess . . . ."

In decision discourse the declarative form may only be used to express what we are sure is true, assuming our intention is not to confuse. Why? *Because 99 plus percent of the time the declaratives we hear and issue in decision discourse are true!** This means then that to use this form to express something that is

---

*While this contention does not come out of rigorous statistical analysis, neither does it come from the blue. There was a time when I listened intensely for the declarative, even recording my phone conversations. The reason I didn't do any formal research is that it quickly became apparent that only a tiny fraction of the bold declaratives I heard in decision-making situations proved to be phonies, i.e., messages that proved to be untrue or matters of opinion. In any case, the research is there to be done. But make sure you are in decision discourse and that you record *all* the declaratives you hear, in particular the enormous number that are mundane: "*It's raining out!* Let's wait a while." "*Monday is Labor Day!* Let's visit my folks." "No, dummy, *that's the wrong key!*

not true or is a matter of opinion is not some additional and legitimate use of the form, but rather a usage that confuses the listener.

Truth is the convention, the rule, and the listener's expectation when he or she hears a message in the declarative form. Countless times when people say such things as *"The movie starts at nine! When do you want to eat?"* "Check with Barbara; *she's back from her vacation!"* and "Hiring Judd is out of the question; *he passed away!"* this is precisely what one will observe if one goes to the movie theater, or goes to Barbara's office, or looks in Judd's casket.

On the other hand, to use the declarative form when one is not certain that something is true is usage that can confuse, frustrate, and infuriate: "You told me the beach was closed!" "Well, it usually closes around this time of year!" "Damn it, it is still open and the kids and I missed a beautiful day at the beach. Watch your use of the bold, declarative form when you are not positive something is true!"

In summary: If I am sure that what I am saying is true, then I *must* use the declarative form, assuming my intention is not to confuse you. But if I am uncertain, I must speak out my uncertainty, which is most often done by slipping in the words "I think . . ." or "In my opinion . . . ."

TROUBLE ON THE HORIZON

A lot of the information that we hold in our heads and that we can legitimately convert into true messages, we have not personally verified. As a matter of fact, often our actual test for truth is not our senses but a *strong psychological feeling* that what we believe to be true is true. In practice this test works an extremely high percentage of the time: e.g., "I have never been to Malta but I *feel certain* it is in the Mediterranean." "I did not actually see the corpse, but I feel certain poor Judd is dead."

So perhaps you can see the psychological problem that is developing here: Because so much of what we *feel to be true is true,* it is only natural to assume that *everything* we feel to be true is true, and to express it in the bold, declarative form and to get furious with those who disagree with us.

Even the political or religious fanatic uses the declarative form correctly 99 plus percent of the time. Most of what he feels positive is true is true even though he has not personally verified it: e.g., where the dynamite is stored, where Heathrow airport is, and what airline will get him to Heathrow.

Nevertheless, a feeling that something is true is not the test of a legitimate declarative. Being verified by our senses is what wins the honor of true, legitimate, nonconfusing, nonfrustrating, and nonmaddening.

And when there is an explosion, speaker to listener, there is a good chance that both feel strongly that what they are saying is true, and both are wrong: it's a matter of opinion.

Chapter Four

The Physical-World Declarative
(Continued)

Physical-world declaratives are founded on . . . physical-world declaratives! If asked the meaning of a PWD, more PWDs are given, each of which can be turned into a picture, in the manner of a child's primer. Thus if I say "It's raining!" and you ask me to explain what I mean, I might issue these PWDs: "I went to the window eleven seconds ago!* I looked out! The sky was extremely dark! I stuck my hand out the window and it got soaked! I saw a steady rain coming down!"

And each of these PWD's can be opened up in turn ("I was

---

*How do you show the passage of time? With a picture of two clocks.

sitting in my chair! I arose! I put one foot in front of the other and moved toward the window!") and the matter taken as far as we care to go, assuming we have some place to go.

A point to be noted and filed away until we get to the desired declarative is that PWDs have no desires in their background argument. The rain is raining regardless of what anyone wants.

SCIENTIFIC VERSUS DECISION DISCOURSE

In scientific discourse a declarative must not only have been verified, it must be verifiable. The listener must be able to observe what the speaker observed. Generally speaking, we must insist on verifiability in decision discourse as well—you must be able to find San Francisco, Malta, and Madison Square Garden where I say they are located.

There is, however, one exception. If I observed something happen, I may—indeed I must—use the declarative form even though I can't prove it happened, assuming my intention is not to confuse you. It is then up to you to decide whether or not to believe me. But there is no way I can qualify my message without confusing you: e.g., "I allegedly saw this happen . . ." or "In my opinion this happened. . . ."

Thus, if you must decide about whether or not to lend Carothers some money and you ask my advice, and if I lent him a hundred dollars a year ago, which he promised to return "tomorrow" and did not return it nor has he yet, then I must say (if my intention is to assist you in your decision) "I lent him a hundred dollars last year, which he never returned!"

I must issue this declarative even though it is not verifiable and even though Carothers has said to you: "I returned the money the next day!"

The point is that one of us has issued a verified declarative even though neither of our declaratives is verifiable.

THE ROLE OF ANGER IN SUPPORT OF TRUTH

We are entitled to our opinions, so it is said, and wisely so since opinion is as common as dust, and life would have ended long ago if we had not developed a tolerance for it. But when it comes to truth we take a hard, dogmatic line with those who disagree with us and often become furious with them. And, by god, we had better become furious.

Whether a street is one way or two-way; whether or not baby has been given its medicine; how much gas is in the plane's tank are not questions that can be ignored, nor can the true answer be compromised if we know it. If, for the sake of harmony, I split the difference between how much fuel I *know* is in the tank with how much you think is in it, we may crash.

People who are are blind (to the truth), crazy (out of touch with reality), or demonic (out to harm us by lies or misinformation) must be set straight, even if it takes a hammer. But prior to a hammer, we can use anger to try to wake them up, expose them, threaten them, and force the truth on them.

Anger sends a message: if you don't agree with me—if you don't change your behavior—then something worse than my anger may follow, including dropping you as a friend, hammering you, or causing a disaster. In short, anger plays the vital role of adjusting the thinking and behavior of those who reject or contradict messages that are true.

So what's the point of all this? The point is that we become just as angry in support of opinion that we believe to be true and that we express in the bold, declarative form. Which is to

say, we look upon people as blind, crazy, and demonic *because
they disagree with our linguistic errors!!*

In the world we create out of our linguistic errors, we end
up surrounded by blind, crazy, and demonic people, even as we
are among their demons.

I have no other world with which to compare this one, but
it is hard to envision a world as crowded, as religious, as armed
to the teeth, and as polluted as this one, where the infuriating
error of confusing truth and opinion is made more often.* I just
don't see how such a world could survive. Indeed, I think it's
touch and go with us as it is.

By contrast, I can envision a world in which opinion is more
recognized and spoken out as opinion and where life is less angry
and violent.

AREN'T THERE OTHER KINDS OF TRUTHS?

Well, in addition to the physical-world declarative, there is the
declarative of pure math ("Two and two are four!"), which we
have set aside, and there is the desire declarative ("This is the
right road!"), which we are about to explore. Other than these

------

*It may seem that I am involved in a contradiction here. In the
last chapter I stressed that more than 99 percent of the time the bold
declaratives we hear in decision discourse are true; now I am saying
I can't envision a world in which the error of confusing truth and opinion
is made more often.

Well it's sort of like those cans of insecticide where more than 99
percent of the ingredients are inert, yet they are still deadly, if not to
bugs then at least to humans. The error of confusing truth and opinion
is not made often, but when it is it can lead to mayhem, a little bit
of which is more than enough.

three declaratives, I know of no other messages that people put in the bold, declarative form *that have any place in decision discourse,* assuming what we always assume, i.e., that we don't want to drive one another mad.

But let's take a preliminary look at these other so-called truths:

Poetic Truths: Certainly poetic truths have no place in decision discourse. It would be infuriating for me to introduce Eliot's bold declarative "April is the cruelest month!" to support my argument that we should not go to England this spring for our vacation.

Intuitive Truths: The problem with intuitive truths—as I have suggested before—is that if I intuit one way and you intuit the other way, we may well get into a screaming match if each of us "just knows in his heart" that what he is saying is true.

Moral Truths: There are such truths but I hope to show in Part Two that they are not a special kind of truth, rather they are *legitimate desire declaratives* and, as such, are verified by our senses.

Religious Truths: Assuming that we mean by this the commandments of God, I shall try to show in Part Two that neither you, nor I, nor any prophet, priest, or person who ever lived could recognize God from the Devil if we fell over Him unless we first knew good from evil, right from wrong. Thus we must already know His truths in order to identify Him, which makes anything He has to say redundant. I conclude that what God is, is silent, leaving us with the exquisite puzzle of how to behave.

Chapter Five

The Desire Declarative

A desire declarative tells the listener the best way to satisfy a desire based on past experience, i.e., how people satisfied the desire in the past.*

There are various ways that we can distinguish a desire declarative from a physical-world declarative.

PWDs make sense even if we don't want anything, e.g., "I-80 links NY and SF."

---

*Technically, all experience is past experience. Still, I use the phrase "past experience" to highlight the particular experiences relevant to the satisfaction of a particular desire—"Past experience indicates that Route 12 has the least traffic!"

Desire declaratives are meaningless unless the speaker has a particular desire in mind: "I-80 is the right road!"

Generally speaking, physical-world declaratives do not have the words "right" and "wrong" in them . . . often desire declaratives do.

Finally, a legitimate desire declarative has two essential elements in its background argument that a PWD does not have: *a shared desire* and *a best option* for satisfying that desire. We find out if these elements are there by asking if they are:

Are we talking about how to satisfy a shared desire?

Based on past experience, is one option our best bet to satisfy the desire?

THE FIRST ESSENTIAL ELEMENT: THE SHARED DESIRE

A shared desire is one that both the speaker and listener(s) have and that (1) they choose to satisfy by cooperating; (2) they can better satisfy by cooperating; and (3) they can only satisfy by cooperating.

Looked at another way, speaker and listener(s) desire one specific future state of affairs to exist and they are cooperating toward this end. For example, the shared desire of John and Marsha will be satisfied if they arrive in Boston at 8 P.M. Toward this end, they are cooperating with one another—pointing out signs; checking the gas, oil, and temperature gauges; and sharing the driving.

When the car breaks down they both desire one specific future state of affairs (that the car run). And toward this end, they must cooperate because Marsha alone has the expertise, but her hand is in a cast, and John, with no expertise, must do the actual work. In short, they share the desire that the car work.

If, after the car is fixed, Marsha wants to stop for dinner, then at this moment she has a *singular desire.* But John agrees with her, which is to say they now have a shared desire, namely, to find a restaurant.

If, after dinner, John wants to stop for the night at a motel but Marsha wants to continue directly to Boston, then they each have *singular and conflicting desires.*

Generally speaking, conflicting desires are settled—when they can be settled—in the name of some other desire, shared or otherwise. John may just give in, compromising his desire to stop for the sake of a desire that is more important to him, namely, not getting into a fight. Or they may flip a coin.

If there are conflicting desires and there is no other desire that overrides them, then we have *raw desires in basic conflict.* This is not necessarily the end of the world. In the case at hand, Marsha pushes John out of the car and goes on to Boston alone. He catches a bus the next day, joins up with her, begs her forgiveness, and they happily tour Boston as planned.

Members of a basketball team share the desire to win the championship. It is always possible, however, that one of the players has bet against his team. To account for such a player—and spies, undercover agents, and saboteurs—I will sometimes refer to the *generally shared desire(s)* of a group.

If half the members of the team want to take an hour off from practice each week to study and the other half does not, then we have *the desires of some* versus *the desires of others.*

A shared desire is a *common desire,* but all common desires are not necessarily shared desires. If all the players want to be team captain, then that is a common desire, but not a shared desire. There can be no cooperating such that everyone will be satisfied.

Closely allied with the shared desire is the *altruistic desire,* i.e., the desire to help someone with his or her decision. Among other things it can result in giving advice, information, or one's opinion: e.g., a farmer giving John and Marsha directions. What they want (to get to Boston) he wants to help them with. For one brief moment the three of them have a shared desire, namely, to get John and Marsha where they want to go.

IT IS ESSENTIAL TO SIGNAL THE VARIOUS DESIRES

Sometimes when we are in a decision-making situation we are talking about how to satisfy a shared desire. Sometimes we are not.

In any case—in all cases—the speaker must be careful to signal the kind of desire he has in mind, assuming his intention is not to confuse, delay, deceive, or infuriate.

- The signal for the singular desire is: "I want. . . ."

- The signal for some of us want is: "Some of us want. . . ."

- The signal for a common but not a shared desire is "I want . . . [to be team captain]."

- The signal for the shared desire is: the bold, declarative form!!!

If—but only if—the desire is shared can the speaker leave out mentioning it. The use of the bold, declarative form conveys this information. Thus, if you and I are in a car and we want to get to Wading River and—after some confusion—I realize that we are finally on the road to Wading River, I don't have to say: "Given our shared desire to get to Wading River, *this is the right road!*" Rather, I can just issue the last five words.

However, if—on our way to Wading River—I am suddenly overcome by the singular desire to take a side trip to the town of Shoreham to see the never-opened nuclear power plant, I *cannot not say,* when we come to the cutoff: "That's the right road!" without deceiving you.

Instead, I must first put my singular desire on the table for discussion: "Hey, I'd like to see the nuclear power plant at Shoreham—the cutoff is to the left up ahead."

THE DESIRE MUST BE A SHARED DESIRE

By what authority do I say that when we use the bold, declarative form the desire must be shared? My authority is common usage and common sense.

Common Usage: More than 99 percent of the time, when we use the bold, declarative form and there is a desire in the background argument, that desire *is* shared or altruistic.

Countless times each day—at work, at home, and on the highway—when someone says "That's the wrong tool!" or "This is the right direction!" the message is founded on a shared or altruistic desire to get the car fixed or to get *us* where *we* want to go.

This is the rule, the convention, and the listener's expectation upon hearing a bold declarative in decision discourse.

Common Sense: If convention had it that we could use the declarative form to express any kind of desire, then after hearing "That's the right road!" the listener would have to ask: "Given whose desire?" And the speaker would have to reply: "Ours, to get to Wading River," or "Mine, to get to Shoreham." And the cumulative delays would be crushing. Indeed, if we did not have a shorthand form to express how to satisfy a shared desire, we would have to invent one.

THE SECOND ESSENTIAL ELEMENT:
THE BEST OPTION

By way of defining some terms, let me tell a few quick stories about students at a parachute jump school.

Paine, who jumps from a plane but has forgotten his chute, is not in a decision-making situation. He has no options. He is compelled to continue along his present course.

Joy is wearing a parachute, and the plane has reached 5,000 feet. She has two obvious options, to jump or not to jump. A nonobvious option might be to ask the pilot to circle around one more time. Obvious options are those that can be assumed between speaker and listener(s). They are, so to speak, on the table.

Joy jumps. She now has only two options: (A) to pull the rip cord or (B) not to pull the rip cord. It has been verified by past experience that if she wants to live, then, between A and B, A is her best option: i.e., in the past more people in her situation satisfied the desire to live by pulling the rip cord than by not pulling it. And this can be verified by jump school records, old newspapers, obituaries, etc.

Is it a sure thing that Joy will live if she chooses option A and die if she chooses option B? No, there are no sure things in real-world decision making. But what is true is that option A satisfied the desire to live more often than option B.

So then, let's put this option terminology to work.

"ROUTE 1 IS THE RIGHT ROAD!"

Imagine that you and I are in a car and that we want to get to Xville. You are the driver, I am your passenger. I know the territory, you do not. We come to a traffic circle of six roads—Routes 1 through 6. I know from past experience that Route 1 goes to Xville and am all but positive that none of the others do.

I say to you, "Route 1 is the right road!"* Is this a legitimate declarative—a truth? It is rather obvious that if my message is indeed true, that buried somewhere in the background argument must be this PWD: "Route 1 goes from this traffic circle to Xville." But what does the word "right" mean? Well, going on the assumption that the message is in shorthand—about as short as possible—we have a sneaking suspicion that if we open up the background argument that "right" can't actually be qualifying "road."

Examine the road as we will (it is made of asphalt, has a white line down its middle, and is heading northeast), the quality or characteristic of "rightness" or "wrongness" never emerges. Roads, like atoms and wrenches, mountains and galaxies, just exist in and of themselves. They are neither right nor wrong.

But there is one thing in the universe that, for sure, does not exist in and of itself, and that is an option!! The very word implies the existence of another option!! Wow!! And that is what "right" (and "wrong") actually modify when we explore the background argument: the right option is the one that satisfies the desire; the wrong option(s) is the one that does not!!!

So the words "right" and "wrong" mean correct and incorrect, given our intention of satisfying a shared desire.

---

*Couldn't I use the imperative form: "Take Route 1!!"? Yes, and I am sure you would not find me rude nor mistrust me if I did. Furthermore, imperatives do save words. However, the point I would make is that imperatives, unlike declaratives, *don't imply that the desire is a shared desire* as those who have been in the army are aware: "Wake up!!" "Forward, march!!" "Column left, march!!" "Column right, march!!" Like everyone else, I often employ the imperative in decision-making situations, but for the sake of our technical analysis of the desire declarative I shall have us exchanging formal declaratives.

Let me try to be clearer for the point is vital: if, based on past experience, people satisfied the shared desire one way more than any other, then that is our best option; and given our intention of satisfying the desire, said option is the correct or right one and all others are the wrong and incorrect options.

Now, once we determined that one option is the best bet for satisfying our shared desire, then we may—like a bureaucrat in heat—stamp the words "right" and "wrong" on roads, people, acts, tools, etc., that will or won't satisfy our shared desire, as in "This is the right road!" and "That's the wrong road!"

This stamping (right road, wrong road) is a helpful shorthand —it saves time—but ultimately only options are "right" and "correct" or "wrong" and "incorrect."

ROUTE 1 IS ONLY A BEST-BET OPTION

Now it so happens that Route 1 is the only road to Xville, so far as I know. So then, is Route 1 a "sure thing"? No, it's still only the best option.

It is always possible that the road has washed out or that a bridge has collapsed and that the best option at present is to park the car and hire a helicopter. It is also possible that in an extremely roundabout way that never occurred to me, we could reach Xville by taking Route 5, and it would be our best option if, in fact, Route 1 has washed out.

To repeat, "sure things" are only "best options."

A CAUTION WITH THE WORD "BEST"

The word "best" must not be taken too literally, since there can be a lot of best-bet options. Assuming that, in all probability,

Route 1 will take us where we want to go and that none of the other roads will, then Routes 2 through 6 are all best options to frustrate our shared desire. I could say—indeed, I must say—of any one of them: "That's the wrong road!"

ROUTE 3 IS THE RIGHT ROAD!"

Imagine now that we are at the same traffic circle but that we want to go to Yville as fast as possible. Both Route 3 and Route 4 will get us there. However, I know from painful experience that Route 4 is generally a horror story traffic-wise, while Route 3 is a breeze in comparison. I would say that 90 percent of the time Route 3 is the best option.

If I have a best option—even if it is not close to a sure thing—then I may still use the bold, declarative form: "Route 3 is the right road!"

Why? Well, if one option is clearly our best bet to satisfy the shared desire, then what other option would rational people pursue?

There is no reason for me to be less than bold or to beat around the bush and go into long explanations as to why Rt. 3 is the right road.

However, I am certainly not prohibited from saying, "Route 3 is usually the best bet."

NO BEST OPTION

If we want to go to Zville, and if Route 5 and Route 6 go there but both routes are known to be horror stories with respect to traffic, then we do not have a best option. Therefore, I cannot employ the bold, declarative form unless my intention is to confuse you. Why not? The usual reason: more than 99 percent of the time the declarative form is founded on a shared or altruistic desire *and* a best option regarding its satisfaction.

If I don't have a best option but a decision must be made, then I have to form an opinion or go with my hunch or intuition. Above all else, I must get out of the bold, declarative form and speak out my opinion or hunch, i.e., I must include the word "opinion" or "hunch."

THE THREE STANDARD QUESTIONS

When confronted with a bold declarative that we are trying to place, there are three Standard Questions we can ask that will help determine whether or not the declarative is a legitimate desire declarative:

Are we in a decision-making situation?

Are we talking about how to satisfy a shared desire?

Has it been verified by past experience that one option is a best bet to satisfy the shared desire?

If, and only if, we get three yes answers, do we have a legitimate desire declarative.

Chapter Six

Truth and Opinion

Imagine that you and I have decided to open a health club with a large outdoor swimming pool. Among the many things we have to do is to hire a lifeguard, and interviewing the candidates is my responsibility. I have no expectations of finding the right or the wrong candidate in the bold, declarative sense of right and wrong. Looked at another way, I feel quite certain that I am going to have to form an opinion about the various candidates.

I am, however, immediately in for a surprise. The first candidate I interview is Roger. Later you ask me about him and I reply *not with an opinion message* but with a bold declarative: "Roger is the wrong person for the job!"

You ask me why, and I give you one element from the background argument: "He can't swim!"

Six milliseconds later the remarkable computerlike ability of your brain brings on screen a dozen horrible pictures caused by hiring a nonswimmer—dead bodies floating belly up, lawyers, the club being closed by the sheriff, and jeering mobs with ropes in loops—and you all but instantly organize the full background argument of my message. You see an easy way to escape this vivid nightmare.

You laugh—in relief—and say, "Roger *is*, in truth, the wrong person for the job! Let's keep looking."

Is my initial declarative true? Let's put it to the Standard Test:

(1) Are we in a decision-making situation? Yes.

(2) Is the speaker talking about the satisfaction of a shared desire? Yes, a lot of them: that no one drown, that we don't go bankrupt, that we don't ruin our families, that we are not looked upon as total fools. . . .

(3) Has it been verified by past experience that, given the two obvious options (to hire or not to hire), one is the best bet to destroy us, or, if you will, to frustrate our shared desires? Yes, the option of hiring; it is the wrong or incorrect option given our intention of not frustrating our desires.

So we get the three necessary yes answers and we have, therefore, a true message: "The hiring option is incorrect, a mistake, wrong regarding satisfying or not frustrating our shared desires, and that's the truth!" And from here we can slap the word "wrong" on the personage of Roger, in a shorthand manner of speaking; i.e., he is the wrong person (for us to hire).

But what has actually been verified? That's a good question. Ideally, a million lifeguards who can swim and a million who can't swim would have been hired over the past ten years. And what would be true is that nonswimming life guards caused the frustration of all sorts of desires while, relatively speaking, swimming lifeguards did not, and that is a truth we would be able to verify in old newspapers and court records.

The fact is, however, that you and I probably don't even know of one instance of anyone hiring a lifeguard who could not swim. Nevertheless, we are not without tons of relevant past experience that can be brought to bear on the Roger situation, including this headline in yesterday's *New York Post:*

FAMILY SUES HOSPITAL FOR TEN MILLION:
'DOC' WAS AN ORDERLY

Even if no one drowns but it gets out we knowingly hired a non-swimmer, we would probably be ruined.

CANDIDATES MOE, FLO, AND JOE

Since rejecting Roger, I have interviewed three other candidates. They all have Senior Red Cross lifeguard certificates and have worked as lifeguards. I am quite certain that none of them is in the Roger category, i.e., a best bet to ruin us if we hire him or her. Nevertheless, in my opinion, they all have serious drawbacks, which I fear will turn off potential members or cause the members who do join to say bad things about our club.

Moe has facial warts with long hairs extending from them; Flo has filthy nails and gummy hair; and Joe has a sinus/honking condition that is in obvious need of medical and/or psychiatric attention. Nor, in my opinion, did any of them display the kind of sparkling personality that can divert attention from physical or even hygienic shortcomings.

I have put them all on hold. I have two other candidates to interview, Allisyn and Clark.

MY OPINION ABOUT HIRING ALLISYN

I have asked Allisyn to stop by and have lunch at my desk. She arrives with two tall cans of Bud Light. She cheerfully offers me one. I shake my head and frown; she then puts them back in their bag and shrugs with a smile.

We talk and she shows me some documents. She has both the Senior and Master's Red Cross certificates and several strong letters of recommendation. She has worked two summers as a lifeguard at the beach. Her brightness, alertness, and wonderful smile beguile and enchant me. I am impressed with Allisyn, but disturbed by the beer. It is not so much that I fear she is an alcoholic. Rather, it is the impropriety—the downright stupidity —of bringing beer to a job interview, no less one for a lifeguard job. I fear for her judgment.

Still, I am aware of no hard evidence that someone who did what she did is a best bet to frustrate our shared desires. Then again, if someone drowned because A. was sloshed or too hungover to see straight, my guilt would be horrendous. Yet, on the other hand . . .

All of which is to suggest that the only thing I feel certain about is my uncertainty re A.

Nevertheless, a decision must be made. You ask me about her and I say, "In my opinion Allisyn is the wrong person for the job." You ask me why and I tell you the good points, but I also tell you about the beer. You think about it for a second and a half and then say that in your opinion the beer doesn't matter that much compared to her obvious pluses over the other candidates. You suggest we hire her but give her a stern warning about drinking on the job.

We bat the question around for thirty seconds, then suddenly you capitulate, compromising—actually sacrificing—your desire to hire her for the sake of other desires that are more important to you: our getting along, returning to your own assignments, and keeping the lifeguard problem in my court. "OK," you say, "but let's settle on someone soon."

THE DREADED UNANNOUNCED SIMILE

In decision discourse "wrong" means incorrect, given our intention of satisfying a desire. However, when I insert the word "opinion" in front of what would otherwise be a bold declarative, *I give a major metaphorical* twist to the meaning of the word "wrong,"* and my message takes on a totally different meaning. The background argument of my spoken message—"In my opinion Allisyn is the wrong person for the job"—goes something like this: "Hiring Allisyn would not really be wrong given our shared desires and compelling evidence from past experience about someone who did what she did, and you, my sane, wise, and decent partner, are certainly not suddenly blind, crazy, or demonic if you disagree with me, but in my opinion hiring her would be sort of like wrong— the incorrect option—in a manner of speaking, if you get what I mean, and of course I could be all wet, as I have been in the past, and she could work out just fine. But then again . . ."

---

*I have used the word "metaphorical" because I could not find an adjective for "simile" in my desk dictionaries. Lo and behold there is an adjective for simile (similative), but since no one I know ever heard of it I shall sacrifice exactly what I want to say for the sake of general comprehension.

If I don't have the makings of a bold declarative—if the past gives no clear direction—but I fail to put in the word "opinion," then I have created the, dreaded "unannounced simile." Instead of "it's sort of like wrong in my opinion" we get—by dropping "opinion" and "like"—"It *is* wrong." The end result is opinion masquerading as truth, which I believe and hope to show has been responsible for more deaths than old age.

BREAKING THE RULES

The first rule of decision discourse is that any rule may be broken just as long as the listener is in on the crime. Depending on our relationship, the inflection in my voice, how I use my hands and twist my face and mouth, I can say "Allisyn is the wrong person for the job" without deceiving or confusing you. I mean I somehow convey that my message, despite its form, is my opinion about hiring Allisyn. But to look you in the eye and say, flatly, "She's the wrong person for the job!" is likely to confuse you if it is not founded on a shared desire and a best-bet option.

WITH OPINION GOOD FEELING
GENERALLY PREVAILS

Generally speaking, when people sense or know that they are in the area of opinion, then tolerance and good feeling prevail. In these situations we often hear or employ such words and phrases as "perhaps," "maybe," "Who knows?" "I don't know," "What do you think?" "It's not a matter of right or wrong," "Let's put it to a vote," "It's a political question," "Let's flip a coin," etc.

Countless times each day, opinions are formed and announced as such and compromises are made and decisions reached without problems. We may not *know* the difference between truth and opinion but we *sense* the difference, and sensing is often enough.

But when we do not sense the difference and do not make the distinction, it can be mayhem, since we end up with opinion that we defend as truth.

NOT MUCH GRAY AREA EXISTS BETWEEN TRUTH AND OPINION

I should probably acknowledge that there is a gray area between truth and opinion, but I am reluctant to do so. If we are in an area that an honest and sane person sees as a gray area, then we are probably in the area of opinion, which is to say that we are not in a gray area.

If we are not certain that the past gives compelling evidence about how to satisfy a desire or if our desires are scrambled or in conflict, then we have to form an opinion or put our desires on the table if we don't want to confuse or infuriate our listener(s).

But let me not be too insistent here. I will agree that if Allisyn had actually drunk one of the beers, that might be considered a gray area, just so long as you agree that, had she brought and killed a six pack, the option to hire would be, in truth and in fact, the incorrect, mistaken, and wrong option.

THE RIGHT CANDIDATE

Is there a right candidate for the lifeguard job, one who is clearly our best-bet option? At the moment I would say no, given the five candidates considered thus far. Roger is clearly out of the question, and the other four are open to opinion. However, in our case we are suddenly presented with a clear best option. His name is Clark and he looks like Christopher Reeve. He has all the Red Cross credentials, has worked at other pools, is intelligent, personable, attractive, and has several warm letters of recommendation.

I say to you, boldly, "We have our lifeguard, his name is Clark, and for sure he is the right person for the job!"

After you interview him, you fully agree with me, and we hire him. Two days after the club opens, someone drowns as Clark looks on in a catatonic panic. Still worse luck for us, it comes out during the trial that Clark had "frozen" once before at another pool, but guests had saved the person in distress and Clark had been quietly desuited. As one witness said with no intention at humor: "He was the perfect lifeguard until he was needed."

Along with the water in the pool, our business goes down the drain. Clark was not the right person for the job. He was, in truth and in fact, the wrong person for the job, given his past behavior.

A QUICK PROCEDURE FOR DISTINGUISHING TRUTH AND OPINION

There is a quick procedure that I have found separates truth from opinion in a great many cases, without having to go into the background argument. What I do is put the word "opinion" in front of any declarative I am trying to identify. If the result sounds odd and jarring, the message is probably true. The mind resists truth being put in the opinion form.

Thus if I say:

"In my opinion arsenic is a poison."

or

"In my opinion Roger is the wrong person for the job."

the results do have an odd ring to them. Arsenic *is* a poison! And a nonswimming lifeguard *is* a clear and present danger to everyone in the pool. These are not matters of opinion.

In contrast, if I say "In my opinion puce is the right color for the reception area," or "In my opinion Allisyn is the wrong person for the job," the message has a proper ring to it—the reason is that they *are* opinions.

Sometimes this procedure won't work because we feel so strongly that our opinion is a truth, that the message only sounds right in the bold, declarative form. Yet even here, if there is a flicker of doubt, and one has considerable patience, the procedure may still work, with some interesting results.

In my own case I took two of my most passionately held beliefs—"Socialism is right!" and "Capitalism is wrong!"—and subjected them to this procedure. Over a period of several years I repeated this message to myself thousands of times: "In *my opinion* socialism is right"; "In *my opinion* capitalism is wrong." Eventually, I came to see both of these beliefs as opinions; I mean I only felt comfortable with them when they had the phrase "in my opinion" in front of them.

In turn, my passion for socialism and against capitalism died. In effect, I changed how I think and feel by deliberately changing how I talked—even though I was only talking to myself.

To those who say I was foolish to think I was anywhere but in the area of opinion in the first place, let me observe: I am not alone; take one of your own most precious convictions and try the same thing. Seriously now, put the words "in my opinion" in front of some belief that you hold to be true about animals or fetuses or all the Ten Commandments and mutter the new message to yourself several thousand times over a period of months, and see what happens.

The most interesting result of this procedure, for me, was that far from leading to moral relativism—i.e.,"It's all a matter of opinion!"—this process revealed some declaratives in the area of morality that sounded quite odd when "In my opinion . . ." was put in front of them. For example: "In my opinion arson is wrong!" or "In my opinion Hitler was immoral!" The reason is that they are not matters of opinion but legitimate desire declaratives, ultimately verified by our senses as we shall begin to appreciate one chapter hence.

Chapter Seven

The Phony Declarative

A phony declarative is any message that arises in decision discourse that is put in the bold, declarative form but is not true. It could be a lie, an unintentional untruth, a partial truth,* or an opinion.

---

*I have not discussed partial truths, in large part because they are even more fascinating than lies, and would require a book all to themselves. For example, take "Men are stronger than women!" There is some truth in this message, but such partial truths are a dangerous business in decision-making situations and they compel nothing. A lot of women are stronger than a lot of men. Therefore the decision as to who should hunt and who should stay home and mind the kids cannot be made based on this partial truth, assuming that we want the strongest people hunting and the weakest people minding the kids. The fact that, throughout history

It is the last phony—opinion masquerading as truth that is my concern because of the horrendous amount of anger and violence it creates among innocent people, i.e., people who slaughter one another with no hope of personal gain. To examine this phony let's return to our health club, the lifeguard question, and Allisyn.

Only in this instance let's put me in the role of me before I saw the light. I mean me when I was so often made angry because I thought and spoke in phonies that I thought were true, and that other people disagreed with. Thus, through my own linguistic error, I came to believe that I was surrounded by fools and charlatans when actually I was surrounded by people with different opinions who were no less sane nor honest than me.

"ALLISYN IS THE WRONG PERSON FOR THE JOB!"

As in the last chapter, I ask Allisyn to stop by and have lunch at my desk. Again she has brought two beers. I frown and, as before, she puts them away. Only in this instance I do no pondering as to whether to hire her or not, because I am immediately certain that, given what she has done, she is, in truth and in fact, *the wrong person for the job!*

Nor did it matter to me at this stage in my life that I couldn't define "wrong," since I truly believed that there was a mighty force in the universe that totally supported my position. So why did I have to know what my message actually meant?!*

---

and across the world, women—regardless of what skills they possessed— have been restricted to the home shows again the compelling power of the bold declarative, whether it is true, partially true, or a matter of opinion.

*Am I talking about God? No, not really, just some final benchmark that would confirm, for any rational person, that Allisyn is the wrong

I had, however, already ordered lunch, and it sat slumped in a bag on my desk, so I opened it; gave A. her cheeseburger, French fries, and Diet Coke; wolfed down my own; asked a few perfunctory questions; and sent her on her way.

Later, you ask me about her and I say "Allisyn is the wrong person for the job!"

This use of the bold, declarative form has the effect of saying to you: "Alert, alert truth being spoken, no room for compromise and if you don't agree with me, you are blind, crazy, or demonic."

You ask me why and I tell you about the beer. I don't bother with A.'s good points. Why should I? Would I have taken up our time telling you how handsome and personable Roger is once I found out he couldn't swim?

You, in turn, are mildly annoyed and slightly suspicious: she *didn't even drink the beer* and you feel I am either making too much of it or have some other reason that I am not revealing.

"Does she have any good points?" you ask.

"What the hell are you talking about," I yell, *"she's out of the question!"*

"That's your opinion," you rejoin, "but let's face it, you just don't want to hire her."

In short, you point out my opinion to me, and suggest ("let's face it") that the beer is not the real or the only reason for my rejection of her.

Nevertheless, this mild response on your part causes me to explode. As usual I am surrounded by fools and idiots!!

I scream: "Are you questioning my integrity!? I have nothing

---

person for the job. I had a heavy religious upbringing but I was cured of religion by the time I was in my early twenties. What I was not cured of—I didn't even know I was sick—was the religious, right/wrong, good/bad way of constantly looking at people and behavior. That cure took years.

really against her. Except that she is the *wrong person for the job!* It is not a matter of opinion! It has nothing to do with what I think or what I want!" (I am, goddamn it, just a spokesperson for the mighty force in the universe.)

Let us assume that your reaction to this outburst is to walk away, saying only (and true it is) "You don't know what the hell you're talking about!"

We are now in the penultimate of bad situations (the worst is coming in a moment). I am innocent (I was not trying to deceive you) and you are right (my bold declarative was actually an opinion).

The argument has escalated from a minor matter (whether or not to hire a particular person) to an extremely important matter—one involving integrity, friendship, comity, and partnership—that could have been prevented if I had only spoken out my opinion *as opinion* or if you had been more sensitive to my linguistic error. For example, suppose you had said the following:

> "My beloved friend and trusted partner, I am slightly annoyed at your misuse of the bold, declarative form re A. I just don't see where someone who did what she did is a 'best bet' to frustrate our shared desires. Stupid? Yes, of course it was.
>
> "But clearly you feel strongly against hiring her, so let's not hire her; but please eschew the phony declarative. It doesn't communicate, it infuriates."

Am I suggesting that we actually talk like this? Sure, why not, at least on occasion? It's fun once you get down the mechanics, and it can get people laughing, which is not a bad substitute for blind fury.

THE WORST SITUATION

In the worst situation we are both hurling phony declaratives at one another.

"Allisyn is the wrong person for the job!"

"Allisyn is the right person for the job!"

This is certainly the worst possible situation since, when it comes to differing opinions, we must compromise. But when it comes to truth we dare not compromise without inviting disaster: e.g., the amount of fuel that I *know* is in the plane's tank versus what you mistakenly think is in the tank.

In short, regarding Allisyn, we are in the area of opinion, since there just is no hard evidence that someone who did what she did is a best bet to destroy us. Therefore the only solution is compromise, which we both feel we cannot do because each of us believes he is speaking the truth.

Nor is this kind of situation helped by my certainty that if I go to the east window, throw it open, and cry out "Am I right?!" a billion or so people, like a giant Greek chorus, would cry back that I am.

Certainly this is the stuff of truth!!

However, you throw open the west window and get an equal number thundering that you are right.

This sensing that each of us has a lot of support for our respective positions—ranging from our momndad to our minister, rabbi, or priest; from school chums to office mates—easily slips us into the belief that what we are saying is true. But the choruses are both wrong. The Allisyn case is a matter of opinion.

SUDDEN AND GRACIOUS CAPITULATION

When the decision is a matter of opinion (because the past does not give clear direction), but the other person is hammering me with bold declaratives, I have found that sudden, sincere, and gracious capitulation on my part can often have an amazing effect on him (or her, of course).

Often he is so worked up that total collapse on my part causes him to fall forward and, off balance, start taking up my argument!! "Well look, don't just give in . . . I mean there is something to be said on your side, I'm not God after all."

Obviously, one cannot go through life always capitulating—nor will the trick always work—but try it on occasion, it's fun and healthy.

PARENTAL TRUTHS AND PHONIES

The endless flow of messages in the bold, declarative form that come from the hearts, minds, and mouths of momsndads are often in a monotonous cadence, a mishmosh of truths and phonies that is impossible for the child to distinguish. They are usually hard for parents to distinguish as well because this is how they got these same messages from their parents, *ad historia redundo.*

So it is that messages—both truths and phonies—get implanted in the child's brain as truths early on. Thus we have parents saying: "It is wrong to play with matches!" "It is wrong to play in the street!" "It is wrong to play with yourself!"

Parents who want to raise unconfused children may say: "It is wrong to play in the street" and "It is wrong to play with matches!" since these are true messages, i.e., they are legitimate desire declaratives. In both cases a shared desire is present (that the kid not get killed) and there are best-bet options regarding its satisfaction, i.e., *not playing in the street* and *not playing with matches.*

However, "It is wrong to play with yourself!" is a phony declarative because it does not have the stuff in its background argument that would make it legitimate. Therefore, the cadence must be broken. Specifically, parents must get out of the bold, declarative form if they don't want to confuse their kid. They may say, for example, "In our opinion you should not masturbate," or "We find masturbation disgusting" without confusing the child.

If they say "It is wrong to masturbate because you will go blind!" then that would be a legitimate desire declarative founded on the obvious shared desire that the kid not go blind. But here the so-called fact (blindness) is not true and the declarative that follows is either an intentional or unintentional untruth—and, in either case, a phony.

The searing into the kid's brain of both truths and phonies at its most formative stage has to cause big trouble down the line. When a child grows up implanted with phonies that it believes with all its heart are truths, and then encounters other adults who have been implanted with contradictory phonies, there must be trouble, since we cannot compromise with truth, or what we perceive to be true.

The choice, then, is either to sort out and reject the phonies of momndad (no easy matter) or fight for all their bold declaratives, as fight we must for truth and phonies perceived as truth, but rejected by other people. It is a nasty choice to pass along to kids.

We are now prepared to explore morality and what passes for morality. Closely associated with religion over the centuries, morality is an extremely dangerous business and maddeningly confusing.

It is quite a digging job, but I hope that, high as the stakes are, there will be some enjoyment along the way, as we sort things out and try to save our ever shrinking planet from linguistic errors and their horrendous consequences.

Part Two

Religion, Morality, and Linguistic Chaos

Chapter Eight

What Is Morality?

Imagine, if you will, that you and I live in an isolated society, a society that is unaware of any other people. It is the universe of human life, so far as it knows. I assume such a society would not have a name—there would be no need—but for our purposes let's call it Alpha.

It is not necessary to think of Alpha as primitive; it is Alpha's isolation and not its level of technology that is important to my argument. Finally, let us assume that you and I, as Alphan's, are concerned with the question of morality; in fact, we have several concerns.

One is the constant pressure from some Alphans to ban certain acts on the ground that they are immoral; acts that are now permitted and that some of us want to continue to have the freedom

73

to do, such as gambling. Indeed, the gambling question is at this very moment getting violent, with the "Nos" screaming in our face that gambling is immoral, that it is robbery, that it is against God's will, and that it is destroying families. And these bold declaratives are now used as the justification for violence. Gambling halls are being bombed, and gambling hall owners and their families are being beaten and killed in the name of morality.

Another concern of ours is that a handful of Alphans—they are known as the supersophisticates—hold that morality is bunk. It is, they claim, nothing more than a mess of murky traditions and ancient opinions that ignorant people hold as truths. Or, as in the current gambling crisis, a case of people using the language of morality to justify their hatreds.

While their numbers are small, the influence of the supersophisticates seems to be growing as more and more Alphans are frightened by the "moralizers." Indeed, buttons have begun to appear with the slogan "Morality is opinion!"

The trouble with the supersophisticates' argument is that if morality is just a matter of opinion, it would seem to lead to an extremely dangerous relativism. Without teaching our children the difference between right and wrong, we might well create a generation of little monsters who would grow into big monsters.

So it is that you and I pursue this question of morality. I, who happen to be unemployed at the moment, am able to put in more time on the question than you, but we talk frequently.

OUR STARTING POINT

Whatever morality ultimately is, it is for sure a word, so we start our exploration here. We listen in on our fellow Alphan's use of the word "morality" to determine if a precise meaning emerges.

THE BELIEVER'S USE OF THE WORD "MORALITY"

In our search we quickly discover that, so far as believers in God are concerned, morality is a set of rules that come from Him. Here is a small sample of these rules: "Thou shall not kill," "Thou shalt not drink alcohol in any form," "Thou shall not steal," "Thou shalt not set fire to thy neighbor's house."

These commandments are sometimes put in bold declarative form: "Alcohol is immoral!" "Arson is wrong!" etc. They have also been incorporated into Alphan law and violators are punished.

Some believers claim that God is against gambling, but here there is a raging dispute even among believers. Indeed, the largest church is at this very moment dividing into two churches over the question.

Finally, we discover, by listening in on believers, that the rules against killing, stealing, alcohol, etc., are the most important consideration in any argument where they are considered relevant. This seems logical enough since the rules come from the highest possible authority. It would sound odd for a believer to say "This act is immoral, it is contrary to the word of God, but even more important. . . ." In short, there is nothing higher to appeal to than morality, i.e., the word of God.

NONBELIEVERS' USE OF THE WORD "MORALITY"

Turning to nonbelievers, we discover something quite interesting. Namely, we still get this same sense that morality is something of paramount importance; the most important consideration, the ultimate guide. It would sound odd for anyone—believer or not—to say in decision discourse, "This act is immoral, but even more important. . . ."

We may no more say "more important than morality . . ."

than we may say "most unique" or "greater than infinity." Buried in the very meaning of the word is this concept that morality is the ultimate guide, the most important consideration.* Since nothing is more important than morality, then everything else—including the law—is less important. And, lo and behold, we do hear people say, on occasion, "This law is immoral!"

Morality's sense of ultimateness is the stuff of day-to-day decision making, justification, and blame in Alpha. Thus we hear it said: "I cannot compromise, it's a matter of moral principle!" "I had no choice but to report him to the authorities. He was making alcohol in his basement; it would have been wrong of me not to report him!" "There can be no justification for what she did; it's immoral! That's all there is to it."

As for the supersophisticates, they seem to be saying that while

---

*In traditional philosophy a distinction is made between:

(1) the familiar rules

(2) the supposed source of the rules (e.g., God, nature, pleasure/ pain, emotion, intuition, custom, the greatest happiness for the greater number, etc.).

But for our purposes I don't think it is necessary to make this distinction.

Day-to-day, the rules are taken as the ultimate guide; philosophically, the source of the rules is the ultimate guide. When I use the word "morality" I shall mean "ultimate guide," with the context indicating whether I am talking about the rules or their source.

One other point while I have you: traditionally, philosophers made no distinction made between morality and ethics. Recently—in everyday use of the two words—a distinction has emerged, with unethical conduct taken to mean something less grave than immoral conduct.

Ethics now seems to be the fundamental rules of conduct *within* a particular profession—politics, medicine, law, etc.—while morality covers the behavior of everyone.

the word "morality" means "ultimate guide," the fact is that no such guide exists. "Morality" is like the word "unicorn"—a word with a precise meaning but representing nothing in the real world. There is no ultimate guide, all is relative, all is a matter of opinion—so sayeth the supersophisticates.

SOMETIMES THE GUIDE DOESN'T GUIDE

As we continue our exploration of morality, we discover something that turns out to be of considerable importance later on, namely, that neither God nor morality guide on all questions.

People often say—without causing disagreement—"It's not a moral question." Even the most devout monk believes that which sandal he puts on first or how he has his eggs in the morning is a free choice, i.e., of no concern to God. This point is important because it suggests that the concept of an ultimate guide—e.g., a divine lawgiver, a supreme benchmark—does not preclude the possibility of situations where it does not guide.

CAN A PERSON REJECT THE ULTIMATE GUIDE?

Another thing we learn about morality, after visiting a prison and interviewing the notorious Bad Pete, is that morality can be rejected. Bad Pete told us, as he dangled from chains in his wretched, reeking cell: "I says to hell with morality, I mean to hell with it!! When someone crosses me, I offs him, and if I needs something, I takes it. And when I wants a little taste, I takes a little taste. So you can take your morality and its rules and shoves 'em, you knows where."

However, another prisoner told us that when he gets out he plans to change his ways and behave in a moral manner. So morality is a decision, an option, a choice.

THE RULES AND THEIR SOURCE

The rules—the prohibitions against certain acts that are called immoral—are certainly real enough. But what about the source of these rules? Is there an ultimate source from which they have been derived, or is it all a matter of superstition, tradition, opinion, and the expression of likes and dislikes as the supersophisticates argue?

Well, let's greatly cut down on the scope of this question by eliminating one possible source of the familiar rules, the one most widely, and mistakenly, believed to be the true source.

GOD CANNOT BE OUR MORAL AUTHORITY

We must now bite the bullet and take God out of the moral picture. Not because of any failure of belief—the reason has nothing to do with belief in the existence of God—but rather because that is how He designed things. Once He gave us the ability to choose between different courses of action—paying attention to what we are told or paying no attention, obeying or disobeying rules and commandments—*He took himself out of the picture.*

He dictated how the ants should behave, but to us He gave this enduring and exquisite puzzle: How should we behave? And He put Himself, forever, beyond the answer. Let me elaborate.

If I heard a voice giving me commands or if I went to the mountain top and a dramatic, spectacular being appeared in flowing robes, backed by thunder and lightening, and handed me a set of commandments etched in stone, the *first choice I would have to make is whether to follow the commandments.*

If the voice or dramatic thing on the mountain commanded me to kill my neighbors, I might well conclude it was the Devil speaking—the voice of evil—certainly my neighbors would.

But if the voice said "Thou shalt not kill!" I might conclude it was God. But in either case my identification of this voice or being is clearly based on *my prior understanding* of right and wrong, good and evil.

The point is that my neighbors and I *use our sense of right and wrong* to identify spectacular beings and to judge the credibility of those who claim to have heard from such beings: good beings or bad beings, God or the devil, true prophets or false prophets.

A crazy person might not do this; he might just obey the voice he hears; but if he starts killing his neighbors, then we either say he is possessed of the Devil, or that he is crazy—and in either case, we restrain him and reject his so-called god.

In short, neither you nor I nor any prophet, priest, or person who ever lived is capable of distinguishing God from the Devil if we fell over Him, unless we already knew right from wrong, good from evil.

Our sense of right and wrong is what we use to separate and identify good and bad spectacular beings and disembodied voices!

Yet even if the voice or thing on the mountain said "Thou shalt not kill!" we could not be sure it was God or a prophet of God. Why? Because it might be the Devil in sheep's clothing, using the do-not-kill commandment to win our confidence toward some nefarious plot involving other instructions. And if it did start giving us more commandments (e.g., no abortion, no gambling), then surely some people would say that it can't be God, while others would insist that it was, and where would we be, but at one another's throats in the name of God.

Finally, we cannot conclude that it was God who put our sense of right and wrong in us in the first place. Why? Because honest and sane people disagree over questions they consider to be moral, and only the Devil himself would have put so many different and conflicting senses of right and wrong in otherwise honest and sane people such that they come to blows and bomb and kill one another over their differences. One person's sense of right and wrong could be in perfect harmony with God's will on all questions, and the senses of all other people flawed to some degree, but how can we possibly tell which is which?

So it is that the ultimate guide—the source of the familiar rules—can't be voices in our head, prophets who have heard voices, or anyone who claims to be in touch with God's wishes. That's how God set it up when He gave us the ability to question, doubt, and make choices. If morality is founded on anything but murky tradition—if it is at heart rational—it is the human mind at work. We are and always have been on our own.

So what, if anything, is the source of the familiar rules? Is there an ultimate guide from whence sprang the rules? That is the question.

Chapter Nine

The Primary Code

We are still in Alpha. I, with more time on my hands than you, have suddenly come up with a theory about the nature of morality and I rush to tell you about it, since it seems to have a direct bearing on the raging crisis over gambling.

"Arson is wrong!" I now see, is true. It is a legitimate desire declarative and entitled to all the honors and passionate support granted all true messages.

"Gambling is wrong!" is a dreaded unannounced simile, an opinion masquerading as a truth, a phony declarative. It must have the word "opinion" in front of it, if our intention is not to drive ourselves mad. Then, speaking out the background argument, we get: "In my opinion gambling is sort of like wrong, in a manner of speaking, if you get what I mean, but you are certainly not blind, crazy, or demonic if you disagree with me."

But let me explain my theory at a leisurely pace, for certainly there is no rush. First, let's wipe the slate clean—freeing ourselves of God, religion, superstition, and mumbo jumbo—and see what we have and where we are led, given what we want.

THE ULTIMATE GUIDE

I want to continue to live; you want to continue to live; just about all our fellow Alphans want to continue to live.

And we need each other.

We Alphans are certainly among those animals least able to survive, naked and alone. Being eaten by larger animals or pack animals is not the least of our problems.

It is possible to imagine us Alphans living on an island without such animals, but even if we did we would have to cooperate to capture and tie down one of our fellow Alphans who had gone mad and was systematically killing people and burning things down, as, in fact, has been known to happen.

So, survival is a common desire that demands cooperation; which is to say that it is a shared desire and, as such, it is a guide to action. *But the shared desire to live is not any old guide to action; it is the ultimate guide!!*

If the survival of Alpha is threatened and we do not make survival our most important concern, then we will die and there won't be any other desires, guides, criteria, ideals, hopes, or principles. We will be dead.

Thus, just as it sounds odd to say "This act is immoral, but even more important . . . ," so it sounds odd to say "This act, if allowed, will destroy all of us, but even more important. . . ."

In short, morality is not a unicorn; the ultimate guide is a real thing in the real world—the ultimate guide is survival.

Am I saying that survival is all there is to life? No. What I am saying—at least what I am going to argue with all my strength—is that survival is all there is to morality. (Oh my gentle reader, I know the wild rebellion going on in your heart at this point, but read on with the wonderful open mind you have displayed up to this point. I am confident you will see in time the terrible cost of making more of morality than survival.)

IMMORAL ACTS

Are there acts that could lead to the destruction of isolated Alpha? Looked at another way, are there acts that, if we Alphans allow *one person freely to wander about doing, or if we allow everyone to do once,* would, in all probability, lead to the death of all of us? Yes. Murder, arson, assault, robbery, and certain kinds of pollution (e.g., poisoning the water supply) are clear and present dangers to the existence of Alpha.*

It is not hard to imagine the end result if we Alphans allowed one person to casually wander about killing people, or if every teenager, as a rite of passage, were allowed to kill one person.

Robbery, arson, assault, and pollution are not far from cold-blooded killing if what is taken, ruined, or harmed is necessary for life, such as food, water, clothing, one's parents, one's dwelling, or the use of one's arms and legs. Even minor acts of thievery

---

*Murder and killing someone; assault and hitting someone over the head; robbery and taking something from someone *are not necessarily the same thing.* But the distinctions can only be made clear when we get to another distinction which comes further down the line: that between guilt and innocence.

could lead to endless violence if they were not forbidden, e.g., life and death struggles over pens and pencils as people refused to be ripped off.

Even if Alpha were a hundred times its current size, a skilled and imaginative person hell-bent on killing everyone could do it, if allowed to go anywhere he wanted to go, and do anything he wanted to do. I mean that, if at some point he was not arrested (in its sense of "stopped"), he could destroy everyone and would, himself, be eaten by a bear, thereby ending the human experiment.

In summary, there are acts that we Alphans *must* forbid in order to survive. I call the rules against these acts the Primary Code or PC. (Rules without penalties are meaningless, but for the moment let's concentrate on the rules necessary to survive.)

MORAL TRUTHS

So it is that the bold declarative "Arson is wrong!" is true. It is a verified desire declarative; a message that gives us the best option for satisfying a generally shared desire. (So, too, are similar declaratives about assault, robbery, poisoning the water supply, and murder being wrong.) It is an awfully short, shorthand message, but still, the arson declarative passes the Standard Test.

(1) Are we in a decision-making situation? Well, if we aren't, let's put ourselves in one: Should we allow people to burn down one another's homes?

(2) Are we working from a shared desire? Yes, to survive.

(3) Has it been verified by past experience that there is a best-bet option to satisfy, or not to frustrate the shared desire? Yes, between allowing such behavior and not al-

lowing it, allowing it is a best bet to destroy us. It has been verified that, in the past, some of our fellow Alphans have burned down homes, barns, and offices, and kept at it until they were caught. Therefore, allowing such behavior is incorrect, given our intention to survive.

Or expanding the original declarative slightly, we get: "Arson is wrong . . . for us to allow!" And that's the truth, if we want to live.

What about the arsonist? Is he wrong to have done what he did? Well sure, in a shorthand manner of speaking. I may certainly say to you, without in anyway confusing you, that he did something wrong [for us to allow]. But keep in mind "right" and "wrong" ultimately modify options, not things, acts, or people.

If the arsonist's intention was to destroy Alpha or his neighbor's home, he was certainly right in choosing arson. I can't think of a better method. The truth is, I don't know what he had in mind, and I don't care. I am too busy helping to track him down.

The arsonist had a decision to make—each of us must make this decision—whether or not to put morality and its rules first. He chose not to do so.

But fear not, there are more accurate terms for the arsonist than "wrong." He is definitely immoral and he may be evil. Immoral: someone who violates the PC. Evil: someone who is dead cold to morality and has no regard for any of the PC rules.

"WHY SHOULD I BE MORAL?"

I think there are two basic reasons, one being as old as the Alphan Bible and the other probably just about as old:

(1) You will be severely punished if you violate the PC and are caught. In the Bible we have the concept of hell; well,

what we do to violators when we catch them can be hell on earth, if not death.

(2) Unless you are a psychopath or sociopath you will probably find the horrendousness of a PC violation hard to live with, even if you are not caught. You have engaged in the kind of behavior that threatens to ruin your life, harm your loved ones, and destroy society; this is a heavy burden for most people to carry. It can cause you not to get to sleep at night and to wake up screaming if you do get to sleep. In short, you can ruin your life even if you are not caught.

FROM TRUTHS TO RULES

If an act is morally wrong, then it must be forbidden. The argument runs like this: Given the desire to live, arson is incorrect for us to allow; and since our intention is to live, we must ban arson, i.e., have a rule against it. The truth that "Arson is wrong!" compels us to ban it, given what we want. A corollary to this argument is that we must allow no one to stand in the way of our banning immoral acts. A tragic corollary to this argument is that if we perceive an act to be immoral—and it is not immoral—we are still compelled to ban it and allow no one to stand in our way.

THE USUAL ROLE OF PASSION AND FURY

Passion and fury support the moral truths and play their usual and helpful role in waking up, correcting, and threatening those who by word or deed deny these truths and violate the rules. However, it is important to keep in mind that this relationship between emotion and truth is not a two way street. We rightly get angry with those who do what is immoral, but everything that angers us or that we hate or find disgusting, repellent, vile, hideous, offensive, reprehensible, shocking, scandalizing, revolting, or annoying is not necessarily immoral.

When we hear the word "immorality" used we must ask: "Are you talking about the end of the world or something that you don't like? If it is the latter then please eschew the word 'immorality,' lest *you* confuse *our* survival with *your* dislikes."

THE FIRST COMMANDMENT

The discussion above leads to morality's First Commandment: *Do not be confused about the nature of morality or you will risk the destruction of everything, later if not sooner.* This Commandment has a corollary: *Beware the unannounced simile!!* (Is it truly wrong or is it "sort of like wrong in your opinion"?)

Indeed, the violation of the First Commandment is at the very moment manifesting itself in Alphan , i.e, the society-ripping crisis over gambling. But before we get to gambling and other ripping-apart questions caused by violating the First Commandment, allow me to expand a bit on the Primary Code and to examine the question of punishment. Oh yes, I shall also tell the tragic tale of Tommy Little, caused by the escape of Bad Pete.

Chapter Ten

The Primary Code (Continued)

Let us leave Alpha for a time and enter the Western world of the nineteenth century.

As it began to be rumored about—and bad boy Fred Nietzsche dared to put the rumor in print—that God had passed away and with Him all codes, values, and moral truths, the role of intuition became increasingly important to moral philosophers and to the person in the street who had lost his or her faith. God might be dead but the intuitive jolt that most everyone got in support of the Primary Code truths could not be ignored. We just *knew* that "Arson is wrong!" was true, even if we could not prove it. As it turns out, we were right and we can prove it.

It is time now, however, to express our appreciation to intuition for helping to get us through a dark time, but bid it adieu. Intuition is too unstable an ally to be counted on, since it also jolts in favor of phony declaratives (messages in the bold, declarative form that are false, partial truths, or matters of opinion). If a moral declarative is true then it has to stand up to the Standard Test for legitimate desire declaratives as, in fact, the arson declarative did. If not, then the message does not belong in the bold declarative form, our deepest intuitive feelings notwithstanding.

RISKING SURVIVAL

Just about all of us take certain risks regarding our own survival. Indeed, we must take risks in order to survive. There are also heroes (people who put the survival of others above their own survival) and daredevils (people who put glory above survival) and people who are killing themselves with work, drugs, and food. So it might be best to acknowledge that there is a certain self-destructive dark spot in a lot of us that scorns survival.

Nevertheless, few of us want others to choose our fate. The kamikaze pilot doesn't want to be mugged on his way to the airport; nor does the highwire artist want to be shot by some clown. Nor do they want their loved ones torched, robbed, or assaulted while they are in the air. Which is to say that both pilot and aerialist are firm supporters of the PC, however cavalier they are with their own lives.

Nor does the workaholic or alcoholic want to be robbed or shot on his or her way to work or a bar. Thus we may account for the hero, the daredevil, and the addict without undermining morality or the PC; both stand firm as Gibraltar.

THE MORALLY RIGHT ACT

Given the shared desire to live, certain acts are right to perform: crying wolf when a wolf is coming, putting one's finger in a leaking dike, and the like. But while PC violations require punishment, acts that are right, good, and correct* don't logically compel any response. It is, however, to the group's advantage to praise, cele-brate, and otherwise encourage those who respond correctly, and, for the most part, this has been understood and done.

But couldn't we punish those who don't do the right thing? Yes. If wolves were constantly on the attack or the dike was con-stantly leaking, there would have to be laws requiring one to cry wolf and to report leaks immediately, and the failure to do so would have to be punished if we were to survive.

PUNISHMENT

Punishment—the word is derived from the Latin for pain—is a strange business. Looking at history and man's earliest myths, it seems that there has usually been hatred of, and revenge against, PC violators. Which is to say that strong emotion has played its usual and constructive role in support of truth, in this case the truth that if we allow certain kinds of behavior, we all will die before our time.

However, if these strong emotions disappeared tomorrow, sur-

---

*Just for the record: Faced with two obvious options upon seeing a wolf: (A) saying nothing or (B) crying wolf, option B is correct and right given the desire that society survive—a matter of primary importance to the girl who sees the wolf. Once we establish that one option is morally correct, then we may, in a shorthand manner of speaking, slap the word "right" on the act, and "good" on the girl.

vival would still demand that we (1) forbid the PC acts; (2) arrest and punish violators. We must arrest and punish for two reasons, so far as I can see: to get the violator out of the way so we can go about the business of living, and as a deterrent to would-be violators.*

Yet this is as far as survival gives us clear direction. It dictates that we do *something with PC violators,* but there is no best-bet option regarding the actual forms of punishment, no proven method for minimizing violations.

So we must form an opinion as to the appropriate kinds of punishment: e.g., ostracism, prison (if so, for how long?), or death. However, mistaking our opinions for truths, we have often gotten into screaming matches, with each side hurling phonies at the other: "Capital punishment is wrong!" "Capital punishment is right!"

Capital punishment is neither.

Given the generally shared desire not only for less crime but for protection of the innocent, neither option seems a clear best bet to satisfy our common goal. Even if we had hard evidence that capital punishment did reduce crime, worries about "wrong person executions" might give us pause. Not only would such a mistake be horrible in itself, but given the right mix of circumstances, the execution of an innocent person could tear a society apart (say along ethnic or religious lines) if his innocence were to come to light after his death.

Observe, then, our situation: morality demands *an* answer (do something with violators) but it does not compel a particular an-

---

*The deterrent effect is hard to measure, but that punishment has such an effect seems indisputable. The looting that takes place after a major disaster seems proof enough that some people will rob when they think they can get away with it. Or, turning the argument around, they don't rob when they think they may get caught and punished.

swer. So the answer we come up with is not *moral truth* (e.g., "Arson is wrong!"), but *moral opinion* ("In my opinion arsonists should be executed"). And like all opinion, it must be expressed as such if we do not want to confuse or be confused by our own words.

In conclusion, then, kinds of punishment are a matter of opinion.

THE RULE OF PRECEDENTS

I have used as my examples arsonists and murderers who keep at their crimes until we catch and stop them. But what about a little old lady who kills her annoying husband of forty years but is in no position to harm anyone else? What should we do with her? Well, I can see mitigating the punishment but not excusing her completely.

If we let her off we are setting a precedent and we don't know what might be triggered in the minds of other little old people regarding annoying spouses, nor would we know what might be triggered in the minds of the friends and relatives of murdered spouses.

Let's now return to Alpha for a time in order to explore:

GUILT AND INNOCENCE

Imagine that you and I are leisurely walking down a country road, on a sparkling clear day. Up ahead, a child is peddling a bike slowly toward us. When the child is about fifty yards away, we recognize that it is Tommy Little, seven years old, a darling boy who has never harmed anyone. The concept of original sin notwithstanding, little Tommy is a prototype example of *an innocent person.* He has done nothing to threaten the survival of Alpha or anyone in it.

Suddenly, a man rushes from the bushes alongside the road and, in lightening-fast order, punches Tommy Little in the face, knocking him off his bike and to the the ground; sticks a large dagger in his chest, takes his bike, and runs down the road away from us. We recognize the perpetrator. You cry "Bad Pete!!" I cry "He's escaped!!" and we run to the sheriff's office.

Now Bad Pete has clearly engaged in the kind of behavior that, if we Alphans allow him or anyone to continue to do, or if we allow everyone to do once, would threaten our survival.

Bad Pete's hitting little Tommy over the head is a perfect example of assault; his killing him a perfect example of murder, and his taking Tommy's bike a perfect example of robbery. In summary, Bad Pete is a perfect example of a person guilty of PC violations.*

---

*Perfect examples, or—if you will—prototype examples, are ones that just about everyone would agree are examples of the thing, act, or characteristic that a particular word represents. Now it is my belief, although I cannot prove it, that all of us hold in our heads prototype examples of words that represent acts, things, or characteristics and that what Bad Pete did to little Tommy matches nicely our personal prototype examples of assault, murder, and robbery.

And what I am trying to get at here is that it is not necessarily a matter of opinion that a particular act (say, the killing of Tommy Little) is, or is not, an act of murder. To argue otherwise is to end up arguing that it is a matter of opinion as to whether the yellow thing before us is *really* a lemon, or Olympic athletes are really engaged in acts of running, jumping and swimming.

On the other hand, if I bumped into you and you took a swing at me and broke my glasses, neither the bumping into nor the swing would fit everyone's prototype examples of assault; i.e., there would be disagreement, and opinion would have to be formed based on what I said ("It was an accident") and what you said ("I thought I was being attacked").

What makes the killing a murder, the hitting an assault, the taking of the bike a robbery, and Bad Pete guilty *is the fact that Tommy Little was innocent.* He did nothing to harm anyone or to threaten the existence of Alpha!! But if either you or I had had a gun and had shot Bad Pete just before the knife went in, or—missing this opportunity—had caught up with him and, gun in hand, had pistol whipped him until we got his blood-dripping dagger from him, these acts would not be murder, assault, or robbery. Why not? Because to do otherwise would mean that an innocent person would die while a guilty person lived to go about his business . . . of murder, assault, and robber. And that is not morality, that is immorality.

So, too, telling the truth and returning what one has borrowed may be the immoral thing to do. Returning an ax to an ax murderer just because it happens to be his, or telling him the truth when he asks where it is, is immoral. It is a case of *Rule Worship.** To come to any other conclusion is to reverse guilt and innocence: the ax murderer lives while innocent people die.

Yes, Virginia, there is a time for killing, hitting, and taking: it is when morality is being threatened, and that is why knowing what morality is, and what it is not, is so vital.

Rule Worship (e.g., *never* lying) is a vicious business that has, over the centuries, been used to sanction the most immoral and brutal behavior. "I'm sorry, but I never lift or throw anything— including life preservers—on the Sabbath." When in doubt, forget the rules and go directly to the shared desire to survive, which created the rules in the first place.

---

*This term is not original with me, but I can't recall whose term it is.

THE RULE OF INNOCENCE

Since it would be wrong to allow Bad Pete to go about his business, so it would be wrong for Alpha or its agents to have harmed little Tommy during his all-too-brief span of years among us.

Looked at another way, we (the group or its agents) must arrest and punish the guilty, but we must not harm the innocent if we can possibly help it. (There are instances where the innocent will be harmed no matter what decision is reached, e.g., not enough food to go around no matter how we slice it.)

This is the *Rule of Innocence,* a rule so essential to our survival that it is nothing short of an instinct with most of us. *The innocent must not be harmed by individuals, the group, or its agents if it can possibly be helped.* It is a rule that carries into all areas of life, not just morality.

If a cop gives us a parking ticket when there is still time on the meter; if a referee calls a penalty when our team is not guilty of an infraction; if we are accused of lying when we have not lied, then, for sure, we will let out a deafening howl.

But if the Rule of Innocence is so widely understood and accepted, why has the history of the real world been the slaughter of the innocent?

This apparent contradiction has a simple resolution: the victims weren't perceived to be innocent in the eyes of the slaughterers. Often they weren't even perceived to be human, given what they believed and how they behaved. "They are savages!" "They are barbarians!" "They don't feel pain the way we do!" "We are superior to them!" "They are primitive!" "They are uncivilized!" "We must convert them or kill them!" "God is on our side!" "They are infidels!" "They are animals!" "They are ignorant beasts!"—and similar phony declaratives anyone of which was considered justification enough to compel slaughter and enslavement, as we have always slaughtered and enslaved animals.

Humans are the only animals that justify and blame. Indeed, most of us feel we can't make a move without justification, and the time spent in blaming could fill half an eternity. Behind our arguments are, as likely as not, phony declaratives which, if we saw them as untrue or matters of opinion, would halt our slaughtering instantly.

Most of us simply cannot get up in the morning and go off slaughtering, we need justification—and what greater justification than that we are right and moral and they are wrong, evil, sinful, immoral, and subhuman. (And to tremendously complicate matters, *they* may be evil, but usually they are not—they are just different.)

That most of the time man has slaughtered in the name of phony declaratives held as truths is the most horrible and tragic thing I know. Killing and killed by linguistic error.

One of these phonies that has caused blood to flow in the streets of Alpha is "Gambling is immoral!" And this brings us to a whole class of killer phonies that have caused oceans of innocent blood to flow since man first made the error of confusing truth and opinion.

Chapter Eleven

The Secondary Codes

Let us, once again, alter our time and place and meet at Kennedy Airport this evening. Allow me, if I may, to blindfold you, put you on a jet, and land you, you know not where.

Without making any inquiries or knowing the language, customs, religion, or laws of the place I drop you, aren't you all but certain that if you killed, assaulted, or robbed the first person you met, or set fire to the first building you came across, or poisoned the water supply, you would—in all probability—be in a lot of trouble if you were caught? In short, if you violated the PC *anywhere* you would, in all likelihood, be in trouble.

The reason you know this ahead of time is not hard to figure: there wouldn't be a society in the first place if it allowed such

99

acts.* However, you would have no idea ahead of time that if you gambled, drank alcohol, did drugs, took up prostitution, tried to buy or sell birth control devices, dated or sought to marry someone of another race or religion, engaged in supra-marital sex, performed or wanted an abortion, took part in a homosexual act, said and wrote what you wanted, tried to introduce a new religion, produced pornography or wanted a divorce, you would be in any trouble or faced with any difficulties.

You might be, but then again you might not be.

These are what I call the Secondary Code acts.

What they have in common is that they are called immoral and are illegal somewhere, but—unlike the PC acts—none are called immoral and are illegal everywhere.

All acts—the PC and the Secondary Code acts combined—that a particular society, religion, or sect calls immoral, I will refer to as its "morality." I will always put "morality" in quotes because I contend that what people call morality—the PC and Secondary Codes combined—is a toxic, linguistic mess, leading as it does to:

(1) laws essential to survival

(2) laws not essential to survival

(3) laws that are a threat to survival

Let us now—remaining in the present and with centuries of wars, rebellions, revolutions, riots, extinctions, and other slaughter-

---

*If I dropped you in Lebanon, you might be temporarily confused as to what you could get away with. You would soon realize, however, that if you were in the territory held by the Shiites, you could not kill or assault a Shiite with impunity. Indeed, a Shiite who kills or assaults another Shiite is subject to the PC and dealt with accordingly, by the Shiites.

ings behind us for guidance—let us examine some of the various Secondary Code proscriptions and the phony declaratives which supposedly compel them.

"GAMBLING IS IMMORAL!"

On the face of it, gambling is no threat to survival. Some societies that allow it are thriving, some that ban it are marginal.

There is, however, the Rule of Innocence to consider. It is not hard to imagine that at some point in time some members of a particular society were genuinely concerned that innocents (children and spouses) were being harmed by a gambling-addicted member of the family: e.g., the rent and the food money was being lost.

Consequently, these concerned people formed the opinion that gambling should not be allowed. Oh, not that it was expressed as opinion (although that is what it was); instead, it was screamed out in bold, declarative form: "Gambling is robbery!" "It is immoral!" "It is wrong!" "It is against God's will!"

And those who disagreed with these phony declaratives were held to be blind, crazy, or demonic and deserved and got a punch in the face or a bomb in the lap for denying the so-called truths about gambling.

But the anti-gambling argument was, nevertheless, opinion; opinion masquerading as truth.

How can I say this if I acknowledge that innocents were being harmed? There are a several reasons:

First, this is a case where the innocent will be harmed regardless of what we do, and in such cases the Rule of Innocence does not provide clear direction.

We may not be accustomed to thinking of gamblers as innocent, but if someone is taking care of his basic responsibilities and if he enjoys gambling, then why—he might argue—should his innocent pleasure be prohibited just because some people get addicted and cause harm to others? Punish them, not me, the gambler might argue.

He might also argue that if we ban all the pleasures that many people enjoy but to which some people become addicted, we surely ban half the pleasures in life. Assuming we don't want to do this, then why single out gambling for banning?

Second, there are other options (besides banning) that are open to a society, including rehabilitation for the addicted, restrictions on the hours and places for gambling, keeping the addicted gamblers out of such places, support for the victims, and media campaigns against excessive gambling.

Finally, there is the problem that banning an act may not reduce it if a lot of people don't think it is wrong, and there is not a substantial increase in police, judges, and jail cells.

If a society is not prepared to arrest and punish all gamblers, then the law should not be on the books.

Why? Because if a lot of people are breaking the law and if arresting all of them would overwhelm the current judicial system, then the cop on the beat will be in a position to pick and choose whom to arrest, which leads to bribery and corruption and, in time, the administration of the PC itself.

In summary, I can see no compelling argument that gambling is immoral. However, this leads to a more interesting question.

MAY WE BAN GAMBLING?

I would think so, just so long as it is done in the name of a lesser criterion than morality that is itself, not inimical to morality. Such acceptable lesser criteria might be the reduction of misery and/or the saving of money.

Why is this seeming technicality—of what criterion we call on—important? Because we must not be confused about the nature of morality, and if there should come a time when some people want to lift the ban on gambling they should not be branded moral degenerates as they would be if gambling were considered immoral. If it is recognized from the start that the ban on gambling is being justified on the reduction-of-misery and/or the saving-of-money criterion, then a lot of confusion and fury can be avoided later.

What I am trying to get at here is that I see no moral reason why we cannot ban gambling and such misery-causing substances as tobacco, alcohol, and other drugs on the grounds that the misery they cause and the cost of taking care of the addicted and picking up after their mess far outweighs the pleasures of these activities and substances.

Yes, as was noted above, the nonaddicted are innocent, but they are also the people who have to pay the tremendous costs incurred by the addicted, and if enough of these innocent people feel they have had enough of the burden, then I see no moral reason why these acts and substances cannot be banned.

However, some lesser criteria are not acceptable to morality. Let's look at to examples: racial and sexual purity.

RACIAL LAWS ARE DEAD WRONG

The evidence is now in: trying to keep the races apart by racial laws is dead wrong. It is clearly the road to death, destruction, the harming of the innocent, and—unless there are reforms—bloodletting down to the last bucket blood of as ever finer racial distinctions are made. (The Nazis made the cutoff at 1/16th—1/16th Jewish blood and you were a Jew—but had they been victorious, certainly the bottom half of the fraction would have continued to double indefinitely until the final pure Aryan was left, and he or she would be eaten by a bear, bringing to an end the human experiment as it pursued racial purity. America had it at 1/8th; 1/8th and you were considered a Negro, which made you 3/5ths of a person.)

Even if the concept of separate but equal were considered possible and everyone wanted it, the inevitable offsprings of white Romeos and black Juliets (and vice versa) would lead to endless and hopeless controversies and third, fourth, and fifth color categories. In time there would have to be a line of water fountains and restrooms as long as a football field. Besides, the decision as to who would ride in the front of the bus would rip society apart.

The evidence is now in: the logical outcome of attempts at racial segregation is a total wipeout, later if not sooner. Racism is immoral!

PUNISHING HOMOSEXUAL BEHAVIOR IS IMMORAL

Since there is no evidence that if we allow homosexual behavior, everyone will become a devout homosexual and thereby end the human experiment, therefore the banning of this act must be founded on some morally acceptable, lesser criterion than the end of the world.

I can think of no such criterion. On the contrary, punishing homosexual behavior seems a clear violation of the Rule of Innocence. Sex is a powerful drive and a great pleasure in the lives of a good number of people—both gay and straight. Yet homosexuals, who are harming no one if they practice safe sex, are being told they must "do it our way, do without, or risk jail, unemployment, and third-class citizenship." The demand seems ridiculous on its face, unless I am missing something.

It is true that homosexual behavior is viewed with disgust

by a good number of people, but disgust is not an acceptable lesser criterion, since who isn't disgusted by this or that? Besides, disgust is an acquired distaste, so one can turn the question upside down and ask: "Why were you trained to be disgusted by this kind of innocent behavior?"

Chapter Twelve

The Secondary Codes (Continued)

Abortion is a horrible question for which there is no answer. There are only horrible answers, all of which are opinions. Aboriton is a prototype example of the insane rage caused by phony declaratives—rage that would be cut by half if those raging put the word "opinion" in front of their messages.

Abortion is also a beautiful and stunning example of people's passionate allegiance to the Rule of Innocence—even though the Rule, in this case, does not apply. People with nothing to gain however the issue is resolved sacrifice their time, their money, their careers, and even their freedom in attempts to save the innocent. The point is, the innocent will die no matter what view prevails; death is inescapable.

If you insist that the fetus go to term, then, sure as history is our witness, some innocent and desperate women will die *along with the fetuses* as they seek and find illegal abortions.

If you allow abortion, not only will fetuses die but you will approach a point where you are terminating sentient beings that are close to human beings by any standard.

In fact, pro-choice people generally—and the U.S. courts in particular—have set a time limit on abortions. This severely compromises the argument that women have a *basic right* to control their bodies and that the decision is one solely between a woman and her doctor. The legitimate expression should be: "In my opinion women should be allowed to have an abortion up to, say, the third or fourth month, but I certainly would not consider you blind, crazy, or demonic if you disagreed with me over this horrible question."

In a similar manner, pro-lifers are severely compromised if they grant abortion in the case of incest or rape. The point being, of course, that the fetus is an innocent, living thing regardless of who the male was.

Is abortion murder? That's a matter of opinion and definition. What murder is—what anything is called—is up to sane people to decide. There is no dictionary in the sky with all the true meanings listed. In most states, causing death by drunk driving now falls under the heading of manslaughter, if not murder, but it didn't used to. Causing death by drunk driving came to be looked upon differently, not because people *discovered* (by looking in the sky) that such deaths *really are murder or manslaughter,* but because sufficient numbers of people and lawmakers *came to the opinion* that it should be considered murder or manslaughter.

It seems to me that pro-lifer's who say "Abortion is murder!" are certainly right if they are talking about abortion after the sixth month, but are totally confused if they are talking about before the third month.

Why? Because they do not consider it to be murder prior to the third month, if they pause long enough in their anger to consider anything.

I have never met a pro-lifer who wants capital punishment or life imprisonment for the woman who has an abortion in the first trimester; indeed, they don't want any punishment for the woman. So the pro-lifers end up with a murder but no punishment, and this, in my opinion, is total confusion—a throwing about of a vital PC term (murder) to cover something they feel strongly about.

Isn't a fetus a human being? That's a matter of opinion, definition, and stage of pregnancy. Personally, I can't get mystical over a few insentient cells. Nor, for that matter, did the Catholic Church in the nineteenth century.

The Church's standard for the *beginning of human life* (according to Laurence H. Tribe in *Abortion;* W. W. Norton & Co., New York, 1990) was not the moment of conception but the moment of "animation" (a Church term, not a medical one).

The Church held that a male fetus "animated" at 40 days while a female fetus animated at the 80th day of gestation. How this distinction between the sexes was arrived at "remains a mystery" according to Mr. Tribe.

In time, the Church changed its *opinion* on abortion, which it is certainly entitled to do. But its new position should not be put in the bold, declarative form, assuming its intention is not to confuse or be confused by its own way of arguing. (That churches invariable misuse the bold, declarative form is my major argument against churches in this ever-shrinking world.)

Abortion remains what it has always been: a horrible question for which there is no answer; there are only horrible answers, all of them matters of opinion.

CAN MORALITY BE TAUGHT?

Yes, I certainly think so. And, in my opinion, it is long past time that it be taught, starting in grade school with field trips to prisons and a day and a night in a cell with horrible screams and moans from the prison population from dusk to dawn. What I am trying to get at here is that the PC and the Rule of Innocence can be taught, and what is done to violators can be dramatically implanted. Furthermore, Secondary Code questions can be discussed and isolated from morality.

RAPE, CHILD MOLESTATION AND INCEST

Rape is one kind of assault. Child molestation is a violation of the Rule of Innocence and is also a form of assault. Incest is the duckbill platypus of morality. It's hard to figure. Generally speaking, incest has been banned and—for the sake of the gene pool—it should be. But it is only recently that anyone knew anything about gene pools, yet the ban goes back to the time of Adam in Eve. As I say, it's hard to figure.

HOW DO WE KNOW IF A QUESTION IS MORAL, POLITICAL, SOCIAL, PERSONAL, OR A MATTER FOR ANN LANDERS?

How do we know that some little, personal decision (e.g., spraying our hair) that is now allowed won't lead to the end of the world?

We don't. And morality wouldn't mind—it it had a mind—if every question and decision were sent up to it for review. That would certainly be putting morality first.

The trouble is that when you make a question moral, there

is a strong tendency to come up with *the* answer when—given past experience and the shared desire to survive—only opinion is possible. But if you call a question political, you are saying, ahead of time, that it is a matter of opinion and open to negotiation.

In any case, the important point is not what kind of question we have, but what kind of answer we can hope for—truth or opinion. Fifty years ago garbage was considered a political and not a moral question. Today it is increasingly viewed as a moral question; if we don't figure out what the hell to do with it and how to reduce the amount we create, we may be crushed and diseased by it.

Nevertheless, fifty years ago opinion had to be formed regarding garbage, and today opinion still must be formed. I believe that today there are a lot more clearly moral questions than there were in former times (particularly those dealing with the environment), but I don't think there are many more moral truths, i.e., firm answers about what to do. For what it is worth, I believe that environmentalists who overuse the bold, declarative form hurt the cause of the environment.

Chapter Thirteen

Alpha's "Morality"

The lumping together of two different things—the Primary and Secondary Codes—under one heading creates a dangerous, linguistic mess that I refer to as a particular society's "morality."

Let us, now, take a closer look at life in isolated Alpha and its "morality."

The economy of Alpha is a fierce barter system that, over the years, has provided some people with lots of gold, jewels, land, crops, and other things to barter, as well as some people with nothing to barter but their broken bodies which don't fetch much.

This system has its critics, but generally speaking rich and poor alike believe that a free market economy is in keeping with God's wishes, He having said to the Prophet of Prophets: "It is wrong to take from another what has been honestly traded!"

While this could be interpreted as simply the PC proscription against stealing, it has been interpreted (by the wealthy and those dependent on their favor: writers, priests, professors, and others) to mean *no taking from the rich to give to the poor.*

However, despite Alpha's fierce economic system—or maybe because of it—most Alphans intuit correctly (re morality) that it would be wrong to allow anyone to starve. Generally speaking this intuition is supported by sympathy for the starving as well. So it is that the wealthy and the better off give the churches food to distribute among the starving.*

---

*For those devoid of this intuition and sympathy, let us examine the background argument behind the legitimate declarative: "It is immoral not to feed the starving!"

If a person must steal food to live, then the Primary Code is being violated in a way that society can and therefore must prevent, namely, by feeding them. To do otherwise is to insist that he die rather than break a rule (no stealing) that was established to help him survive in the first place, and this would be a case of Rule Worship and nonsense.

But suppose the starving person is too weak to steal? We still must feed him because, even if he is too weak to speak, he is, in effect, asking a question to which we must give a yes or no answer: namely, "Will you feed me?"

If we say no (or turn our backs) then we are subjecting innocent people to what is identical to the worst form of punishment (death) without any crime having been committed. This would be a clear violation of the Rule of Innocence.

It is possible the starving man is not considered innocent—"Serves him right, he never worked a day in his life"—but letting him die is certainly too harsh a punishment in my opinion, although I can see where it might be argued in a society existing on the edge of survival.

In the most desperate situation of all—when there is not enough food to go around—then innocents will die no matter what is done. In such a case, neither morality nor the Rule of Innocence gives clear direction, and all we can do is form an opinion.

The political system of Alpha is, shall we say, a "limited democracy." The enfranchised enjoy freedom of speech, freedom of assembly, and freedom of religion. These rights are part of Alphan "morality." In other words, they are not considered political rights that the enfranchised have granted themselves, but rather rights that come from God and nature, i.e., God-given, natural rights.

Those who are not enfranchised do not have these rights. This exclusion is also believed to be in keeping with morality and divine and natural order by those who have these rights, and it may not be denied (with impunity) by those who do not have these rights.

In particular, the women are not enfranchised, and none of the rights enjoyed by the men are granted to them. Nor can the women complain (with impunity), since they don't have the right to complain. Indeed, the women are treated like property and even less than property: divorced at will, confined to the home, and beaten by their husbands with impunity.

For most women, however, there is no daily physical punishment. Like the men, the women are inculcated with the Secondary Code and the phony declaratives on which it is founded ("Women are inferior to men!" "A woman's place is in the home!" "Women are the servants of God's servants!") and most of them comply with Alpha's "morality." Furthermore, many of those who do comply are loved and treated kindly.

Alcohol is considered immoral; it is illegal and there is general compliance with the ban. Homosexual acts are common, particularly on hunting trips and at the baths. Pornography is allowed and is relished.

Lesbian behavior is considered extremely immoral and is punishable by death. A daughter who engages in premarital sex may be killed by her father, and an unfaithful wife may be killed by her husband—i.e., killed with impunity. Generally speaking, the man involved with the woman is considered a victim and is not harmed.

There is, however, an ambivalence to the treatment of "fallen women." If a daughter or wife can escape the wrath and the house of her father or husband, she is allowed to slip into prostitution, which is not considered immoral and is not illegal.

The treatment of women is not only believed by the men to be morally correct, but such is the mixture of the Primary and Secondary Codes into a single, powerful brew that one cannot say—and be accurate—that in their treatment of the women, the men are guilty of hypocrisy, narrow self-interest, self-indulgence, insincerity, or deceit.

The point is that an Alphan woman who gives up her virginity prior to the blessing of marriage, or who talks back to her husband, is truly perceived by the men as the worst Primary Code violator is perceived, i.e., as a threat to everything, since the men intuit from the depths of their being that without morality all is lost. And this intuition is partly correct, for buried in the mess that is Alpha's "morality" is the PC, without which all *is* lost.

None of this is meant to suggest that the men are not guilty. Their original sin is linguistic confusion, leading to the creation of phony declaratives, leading to a violation of the First Commandment (don't be confused about the nature of morality), leading to exclusion of women from the PC protections, leading to brutal and immoral treatment of women. In short, linguistic error has created a "morality" that is immoral.

Do I really think this is the source of the treatment of women? Definitely!! For without belief in the phony declaratives on which Alpha's Secondary Code is founded ("A woman's place is in the home!" etc.), and the passionate belief that these phonies are true, then the Secondary Code proscriptions collapse and Alpha is left with the Primary Code, which does not allow for assaulting anyone.

Nor is one faced with the task of proving that women are equal to men in order to undermine the way Alphan women are treated. All you have to say is: "In my opinion women are equal to men and should be treated equally." This causes the other person to scream that it's not a matter of opinion, even as the fact that it is a matter of opinion is beginning to sink in, in the audience. In time, the audience laughs at the screamer; he looks ancient, out of touch, foolish. Or so it has been my experience with tossing in the word "opinion."

All this aside, the women of Alpha are now brutalized if they don't conform with the Secondary Code proscriptions. Yet despite this immoral behavior against the women, Alpha survives. It survives because "institutional immorality"—immorality built into the very laws and customs of society and administered or sanctioned by the same people who administer the Primary Code—can last a long time without destroying a society.

The reason is twofold: (1) the institutionalized immorality is strictly limited (a given man may only attack his own wife and daughter), and (2) the women generally comply and therefore survive. But sooner or later the piper must be paid. A society that lives in violation of the First Commandment is, in effect, living on the side of a volcano. It may lie dormant for centuries or *explode tomorrow as some difference of opinion gets tagged moral, and people go crazy.* Such as—and for example—the question of gambling, which overnight has become a raging and violent "moral" issue within Alpha.

Perhaps even more threatening to the survival of Alpha are the Secret Sisters whose movement is growing and who have on their agenda for consideration poisoning the enfranchised and educating male children differently.

Chapter Fourteen

Catastrophe!

Let us now leave Alpha and travel east, west, north, or south—travel, in any case, until we discover another society, one like Alpha in that it is isolated and unaware of other people. Let's call it Omega and examine it quickly.

Omega has both the PC and a Secondary Code. However, no distinction is made between the two since none is recognized. The PC is the same as Alpha's; the Secondary Code, however, is different in many respects, which is to say that a lot of what Omega calls immoral Alpha does not, and vice versa. As with Alpha, the strongest emotions support Omega's "morality" (i.e., both codes).

Omega's government is a monarchy and its economy is feudal. There is no social, political, or economic discrimination against women. All work is shared—at least among the peasants—and, as often as not, the monarch and the ministers have been women. The monarch is subject to the will of God but no one else.

Premarital sex is allowed and is common. Infidelity is winked at, and the aggrieved party may not harm the aggrieving parties beyond calling them bad names. Prostitution is considered immoral and is illegal. Both parties are punished. Alcohol is permitted and there is a lot of drinking. There are many holidays and the pace of life is leisurely by comparison with Alpha. Gambling is allowed during the holidays, but not otherwise.

There is a court censor, and works considered offensive to the Crown are prohibited and writers and artists may be punished. Pornography is not allowed.

Most Omegans consider homosexual acts immoral in the extreme and there are harsh laws against them, including death for second offenders. Those who are even suspected of homosexual behavior are harassed, assaulted, and even killed by ordinary citizens, with impunity.

Thus, as with Alpha, Omega is guilty of institutional immorality. The very people who administer the PC are guilty of violating it and allowing others to violate it.

Nevertheless, life goes on in Omega and for the same reason it goes on in Alpha: the institutionalized immorality is controlled and limited, i.e., only homosexuals may be assaulted and killed with impunity. Furthermore, as with Alpha, there is general compliance with the Omegan "morality," limiting the number of assaults against, and murders of, homosexuals.

In short, the volcano that is Omegan "morality," slumbers. But the First Commandment will win out!! People who live in moral confusion are on the road to destruction, sooner or later, unless there are reforms that bring society in line with the demands of morality and the Rule of Innocence.

And lo and so it comes to pass that, suddenly, all hell breaks loose, even as morality promises if The First Commandment is violated.

Suddenly there is a mind-ripping explosion that—as it is repeated elsewhere throughout the (real) world—forever alters humankind, and raises the specter of extinction. The true king of the beasts may, in the final analysis, be destroyed by the very thing that made us king of the beasts—language. (The dumb animals purr and pant at the pleasing prospect.)

What happens is that Alpha and Omega become aware of one another. Do they rush into one another's arms and cry: "Brothers and sisters, isn't it amazing—we have never met before yet we both have the same set of moral rules, as all human beings must if they are to survive!! All hail humankind, all hail universal morality, all hail the Primary Code, without which there is nothing!'"?

Hardly. Indeed, they don't even notice what they have in common since they are overwhelmed by what they don't have in common.

More to the point, what they see in the other group is frightening, horrendous, disgusting, and revolting. And what each side expresses is raw loathing: "Sodomites!" "Whores!" "Brutes!" "Murderers!" "Adulterers!" "Oppressors!" "Moral degenerates!" "Sexual deviates!" "Fornicators!" "Vicious sexists!" "Perverts!" "Animals!" "Monsters!" "Drunks!" "Ogres!" "Beasts!" "Pigs!" "Dogs!" "Rats!" "Skunks!" "Vermin!" "Snakes!" "Scum!" "Homos!" "Fags!" "Flits!" "Sluts!"—the same raw loathings they have toward those in their own societies who violate "morality"* only now each side sees an entire people who are subhuman, given what they allow and how they behave.

They see strangers, aliens, foreigners—the very words causing

---

*To complicate matters terribly, each side also sees *true* immorality on the other side, i.e., the brutalizing of women in Alpha, the brutalizing of gays in Omega. What a mess.

one's flesh to creep. To have a group that behaves in such a way outside one's borders is as dangerous as having a person who behaves in such a manner inside one's borders. Who knows what such horrible and immoral people are capable of? Each group must prepare for battle against infidels, i.e., those who do not believe in the right, the good and the truth.

At this traumatic point in time we enter what I call the Second Stage of human history. I have in mind the time between the first awareness of other peoples and 1945. This Second Stage was a horrendous period for morality; the constant, endless, and massive slaughtering of one nationality by another was in my opinion, more significant than what was discovered, invented, created, or built.

I say more significant because if we finally do self-destruct then an Extraterrestrial grad student, landing on planet Earth and sifting through old clips and T.V. tapes, might find our accomplishments far less significant than our linguistic errors. We may become an intragalactic case study of the danger of the phony declarative, a planet more concerned with purifying belief than the air.

Throughout the Second Stage, morality's caution remained the same. "Do not be confused about the nature of morality or you will risk the destruction of everything." Yet it was a peculiar time, this Second Stage. Some people did argue that nations should act morally, but it was, at best, a soft argument. There was no morality between nations and there were mass slaughterings, yet life went on contrary to the promise of morality that life would end if people wandered about killing and torching. It went on because distances between peoples were long, weapons were crude, and there was—institutional immorality notwithstanding—the administration of the PC *within nations*. And this rough administration of the PC allowed the fodder to constantly regenerate.

Historians—puffed with terms such as "realpolitik" and "lebensraum" (room to live)—claimed to see through the rhetoric by which leaders led people to slaughter during the Second Stage.

They (the historians) claim to give us *the real story*—grabs for land and resources—but in doing so they miss the real story, in my opinion. Grabs for land and resources never meant much to those doing the actual killing and dying. They knew enough history to know that after the battle they would have nothing more (if they lived) than before the battle. Maybe a humble pension for a lost limb or two, or a little flag to wave on Veteran's Day, but beyond that nothing, nor was more expected by the fodder of the country.

The real story, as I see it, has always been in the minds and the hearts of the followers. We believed in the just cause, in having right triumph and evil destroyed. We believed the phony declaratives we were fed.

Crude, dirty, and rough-hewned as we were, we believed in God and in His rule. We believed we were on His side. We believed that our country's morality was best, and the moralities of all other countries were worse, much worse. We answered the call to duty as defined by king, pope, mullah, and prophet.

What man or woman among us would run off and slaughter or risk slaughter without the support of bold declaratives that we believed to be true: "We are right!" "They are wrong!"? Let a leader put certain words together in a bold declarative—"right," "wrong," "God," "country," "duty"—and the lifetime miser throws his savings on the table to equip his child for battle death.

Since every country's Secondary Code was different from every other country's, therefore everyone was immoral in the eyes of everyone else, and there was plenty of righteous work to be done. Every country was surrounded by immorality. There were always battles to be fought; crusades to be undertaken; new lands to be civilized; weaker people to be colonized; infidels to be converted;

burdens for the white man to bear; evil to be confronted; and subhumans to be enslaved, killed, converted, and plundered for their own good or the benefit of God, Crown, and State.

Every school child learned that Balboa *discovered* the Pacific Ocean. "Balboa discovered the Pacific Ocean in 1513!" . . . it is really too much, when one comes to think about it. What a colossal arrogance, a contempt for masses of people and caused by a handful of phonies passed down from parent to child: "We are civilized, they are primitive!" "We are in harmony with God's wishes; they are pagans!" "We are superior to everyone else!"

So it was during the Second Stage.

Then at last came the Third Stage with the blessing (in 1945) of the Atomic Bomb. At last morality was vindicated and things began to improve rapidly from a moral standpoint.

Am I kidding? No. You are overwhelmed by the immorality that exists in the world. That's fine, that's great, but unless you recognize the fantastic moral progress made during the the the past 45 years over the preceding 4,500 years, you will be immobilized by your cynical view and remain unable or unwilling to help move us on to the Fourth Stage, if there is to be one: the community of nations guided by the PC.

Since 1945 there has been a tremendous change in words, attitudes, reactions, and behavior on the planet and in the direction of morality. No longer does one hear of the "white man's burden" or hear much of "the colonies" or "empire." It is true that religious fundamentalism is a big threat and reminds us how far we have to go, but the reason fundamentalism is even noticed today is that the whole world used to be fundamentalist, which meant that fundamentalism—like the air when it was clean—was unnoticed. Today fundamentalism is seen as the terrible threat it is to morality, i.e., survival.

The list of human rights violations (or as I call them, institutional violations) is long, but that such lists are kept and all countries that commit such violations deny that they do, is unique in the history of the world.

Half the world's population—the female half—now has standards to aim for, which did not exist half a century ago. Neither weapons nor oil will help the shieks, sultans, princes, and emirs when our Arab sisters drop their veils and see the light.

Ten thousand gays marching together is no longer the standard by which the media considers coverage, it takes 100,000 at a minimum.

Increasingly, racism is seen as a world evil, an extremely dangerous business. Few military heroes ever received the outpouring of respect and affection that Nelson Mandela received.

The behavior of the people in Northern Ireland, Lebanon, and Angola is looked upon as an embarrassment to the human race—something we would steer an Extraterrestrial clear of should it visit our planet. Iran and Iraq were properly considered genocidal, homicidal, and crazy as they crossed an imaginary line which is their mutual border like a child's game of dare played with real children. It makes one sick.

Muammar Qaddafi is seen as an outlaw even by nations he hasn't troubled. Saddam Hussein knocks over a filling station owned by a rich guy and the world sees it as a PC violation, and for the first time in the history of the world, the world unites against one of its members. And the world is right; the PC sets no income limit on the victims of robbery, assault, and murder.*

---

*That George Bush singlehandedly made the U. S. Globocop raises serious questions for the world and for the United States as well. But that morality demands a cop, a judge and punishment if it is to be anything more than wind seems obvious. Maybe, if things work out, we will look upon this period of world history as the American west looks on its history. First there was the self-appointed, gun-slinging sheriff followed, in time, by civil-service cops under civilian control. As I write these words Saddam has just dumped the oil in the Gulf, an act that

Communist regimes collapse all over the place and there is surprisingly little celebrating in the West. The new regimes are seen as our relatives and we see their troubles as our troubles— a burden not joyously taken but taken nevertheless. We in the West will try to help them.

But far and away the greatest sign of moral progress is that two giant mortal enemies—their borders separated at one point by only eighty miles of water—did not go to war with one another over a 45-year period. Certainly that is a record for giant, mortal enemies in the history of the planet.

Morality will be heard, morality is being heard and accepted at last between peoples. The justifications for all the immorality in the name of morality are slowly withering across the world.

We can thank the bomb for this progress. It forced the giants not to fight with one another and weakened their atavistic colonial instincts to such a degree that the battles they fought with former colonies ended in political messes and defeats. The giants were confused and muscle-bound by the bomb.

From morality's view there has been great progress, given the way things used to be, but are we progressing fast enough? If we don't further split truth from opinion and the PC from the Secondary Codes; if we don't get more moral and less "moral"; if we don't come to see the planet as a community; if we don't stop propagating at the current rate; if we don't get religion out of our damn hair; if we don't cut back armaments; if we don't stop ripping up the environment; if we don't help the workers living off the ripping up, I don't think there will be a Fourth Stage, a Stage of a moral planet. Yet I believe there could be.

Never in the history of the world has there been an opportunity

---

is immoral but not illegal. Will we make it illegal, and, if we do, what will be the punishment? In short, we have a lot of heavy thinking ahead of us.

for a leader to call people to a truly noble cause—serving morality, serving survival.

Yet it is a call that no leader makes, for all people want are cars and VCRs.

Besides, there is no money.

In my opinion, those who make this argument don't know history, money, or people. History is the story of the noble cause; men and women throwing off selfish and petty concerns to run off to to serve God and country.

What difference would it make now to work for the glory of the planet?

Money? We are in such a relentless and faithful habit of spending incalculable sums on military personnel and weapons that minor planet-wide adjustments would free up billions for cleaning up, for birth control propaganda and devices, for food, for medical care, etc.

Marching forward as if to war with the word opinion happily on our lips, worried always about the little guy who makes his or her living cutting down trees or making weapons; laughing, friendly, helpful, it will just take the call. If you will make it, I will follow. I am a humble scrivener, not a leader, but I shall scriven for you, remembering—for it is my specialty—that it is more important *how* we argue than *what* we argue. Let's go!